BRITISH POSTERS

OF THE FIRST WORLD WAR

BRITISH POSTERS

OF THE FIRST WORLD WAR

John Christopher

Recruiting Sergeant. "Now, I can tell character when I see it, so mark my words. If you join now you'll be a swankin' general in five years."

A pre-war cartoon from *Punch*, published in March 1914.

Recruiting Sergeant: 'Now, I can tell character when I see it, so mark my words. If you join now you'll be a swankin' general in five years.'

First published 2014

Amberley Publishing
The Hill, Stroud,
Gloucestershire, GL5 4EP

www.amberley-books.com

ISBN 978 1 4456 3316 9 (hardback)
ISBN 978 1 4456 3330 5 (ebook)

British Library Cataloguing in Publication Data.
A catalogue record for this book is available from the British Library.

Typesetting and Origination by Amberley Publishing.
Printed in Great Britain.

Contents

Fresh-faced and khaki-clad, 'Kitchener's men on a route march'. (J&C McCutcheon Collection)

Introduction

Kitchener's Army came into existence with a rush. It came into existence in the crowded streets of the great cities, in the peaceful villages up and down England, Scotland, Ireland, and Wales, where men came forth from office, warehouse and factory, or tramped from their farms and their cottages to the nearest recruiting office, it came into existence on the decks of homeward bound steamers, where little coteries of young men, eager and enthusiastic, returning to their Motherland to give their services, had already joined themselves into parties for enlistment in certain regiments.

Edgar Wallace, *Kitchener's Army*

Change of Use
At the outbreak of the war the London offices of the Hamburg–America line were transformed into a British Army recruiting office. It is interesting to note how many of the smaller posters are without illustrations at this early stage. (J&C McCutcheon Collection)

At the outbreak of the First World War, or the Great War as it was generally termed at the time, Britain's confidence in its naval superiority and the protection offered by its waters had left the nation unprepared for a drawn-out land war. The Army consisted of around 710,000 men including reserves, of which only 80,000 were regular troops, trained and ready to fight. This was far less than either the German or French armies. The British Army was made up of six divisions and one cavalry division within the UK, and a further four divisions overseas. There were also fourteen Territorial Force divisions, plus 300,000 men in the Reserves. The Secretary of State for War, Lord Kitchener, feared that the untrained Territorials would be ineffectual and despite the popular feeling that it would be 'all over by Christmas', he anticipated a far longer and more drawn-out war. More men and, as the posters would later state, yet more men were needed. However, the British had an established policy of not using conscription for overseas conflicts, and at first all of the extra men were volunteers, encouraged to enlist through the persuasive propaganda of the time and, in no small measure, by the countless recruiting posters that beckoned and pointed on every street, as well as the peer pressure from friends, colleagues and family.

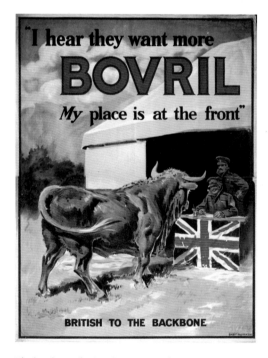

If the boundaries between advertising and recruiting posters were blurred at times, the advertisers also incorporated elements of the recruiting posters in their adverts, making it difficult to tell which was which. These two examples feature a Bovril bull attempting to enlist, and Sunlight soap making the British Tommy 'the cleanest fighter in the world'. All very patriotic, but they are, quite blatantly, advertisements aimed at selling products.

DERBY'S DAY.

WITH MR. PUNCH'S COMPLIMENTS TO THE DIRECTOR OF RECRUITING.

If you think that cartoons were solely intended to be humorous, think again. Many were highly political, such as this *Punch* cartoon from November 1915. The Derby scheme gathered men to 'attest' to serve if called upon.

Derby men handing in their armlets at White City Central Depot in exchange for full uniforms. (J&C McCutcheon Collection)

In an age long before television, the posters were the most immediate means of mass communication available, especially with their target audience – the mostly illiterate or semi-literate men of the working classes – who did more than their share to feed the machinery of war. Advertising posters were well established throughout the towns and cities, and while the British posters might have lacked the artistic qualities of their French counterparts, or the graphic boldness of the German posters, their slogans and simple imagery were easily and instantly understood by the general public. Through this extensive collection of posters it is possible to explore the themes that emerged throughout the course of the war years. For the initial period they were fairly innocuous appeals or calls to action, inviting the men to enlist, to 'answer the call'. It was all about duty and pride as the flow of civilians seamlessly became ranks of khaki-clad soldiers. Smiling faces abounded beneath slogans such as, 'Come along boys!' Another featured a smiling Tommy and the words, 'He's happy and satisfied – are you?'

An initial wave of enthusiasm saw 750,000 men enlist by the end of September 1914, rising to a million by the end of the year. Their reasons for joining up were many and varied and while no doubt some were prompted by unemployment and poverty at home, the recruiting boom did not subside in the wake of the British retreat following the Battle of Mons. Clearly the war was not going to be over by Christmas and, despite the cheeriness of the poster images, it had become a grim and dangerous business. Many men joined up precisely because they perceived that the dangers threatened their homes and their country. The general sense of patriotic fervour was heightened by the appearance of certain emblems of nationhood on the posters, most notably the Union Jack, the king – although to a lesser extent – and a most unlikely poster icon in the form of the moustached Secretary of War, Lord Kitchener (see page 41). As the war progressed the poster makers increasingly employed basic psychological ploys, working on several levels by tapping into a sense of guilt. 'Are you in this?' they wrote, the inference being, 'then why not?'

When viewed as a whole, the British posters seem remarkably tame. The conditions at the Front and the reality of fighting or dying were seldom represented, although the atrocities of the enemy – the shelling of Scarborough, the Zeppelin raids on civilians and the sinking of the *Lusitania* – did convey something of the horrors of the war. But above all else, the posters are unexceptional in execution and convey no sense of a cohesive campaign on the part of the authorities, and that is exactly how it was. The body that coordinated the posters, the Parliamentary Recruiting Committee, was made up from many political parties. Its main role was to use the party organisations for recruiting purposes, distributing the posters and circulars and organising events. Designs for individual posters would be submitted by the printing companies for approval by the committee, and the artwork was prepared by the printer's own artists or draughtsmen. As a result the recruiting posters had much in common with the peacetime advertising posters, and it is said that this gave them 'working class appeal'. In contrast, the posters of the innumerable charitable committees set up during the war were commissioned by middle-class patrons from well-known artists of the day, such as John Hassall and Frank Brangwyn.

Men queue outside the recruiting office. Some wear straw boaters and bow ties, most are wearing flat caps. (J&C McCutcheon Collection)

In many cases there was a cross-fertilisation of designs, and the more politically edgy cartoons of magazines such as *Punch* were often turned into posters, although in a few cases this process was turned the other way around, with the posters inspiring the cartoonists. As will be seen in many examples in this selection, designs and concepts were frequently reused, either in modified form or adapted into new designs, and an individual design might appear in several formats and sizes. Thoroughly British they might be, great works of art they were not. Nonetheless, the posters of the First World War have left us with many enduring and iconic images that remain in the public consciousness to this day, a century later.

Were the recruiting posters effective? It is hard to say. The demand for men remained constant and new appeals were issued, along with a succession of schemes such as that of the Pals Battalions, a scheme which was devised to encourage groups of men to join up together – an idea first suggested by Lord Derby. By late 1915, a year into the war, around 2.5 million men had enlisted and a further 1.5 were in reserved occupations. A National Registration Act passed that year saw all eligible men registered, and in early 1916, the Military Service Act saw the introduction of conscription for men aged between eighteen and forty-one. This largely put paid to the recruiting poster as such, but other posters continued to appear on the Home Front, providing information and advice to help the war effort as well as recruiting an army of volunteers to carry out essential war work – many of them women – or selling war bonds for munitions and raising money for charities. A selection of Home Front posters is included towards the end of this book.

The main bulk of the posters published here come from the collection of the US Library of Congress. By no means definitive, it is, however, a comprehensive selection that reveals the evolution and variety of posters of the First World War.

Marching Off to War
There's a simple inevitability about joining the column of marching soldiers, each with a song and a smile on their faces. On the opposite page, this poster for the 2nd City of London Battalion Royal Fusiliers offers 'Uniform & Necessaries Immediately on Enlistment' in addition to 'Army Rates of Pay & Allowances'. The two examples on this page reinforce the ease of transition from civilian life to a place in the ranks. 'Don't stay in the crowd and stare. You are wanted at the Front.' The idea of the types of headgear reflecting a range of backgrounds and occupations is depicted in more graphic detail, *below*, with carpenter, lawyer, farmer and artist amid the throng. In these early posters there is no subtext or attempt to coerce men into signing up, instead they rely on the most basic motivation of doing one's duty and answering the call.

'Answer the call.' Poster for the London Rifle Brigade.

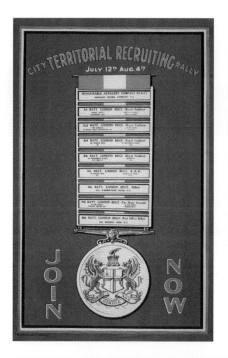

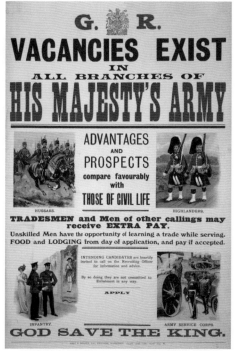

Four more London posters. *Top left:* City Territorial recruiting for a number of London regiments. *Top right:* Looking like a promotion for a fashion parade, this poster for the Coldstream Guards pre-dates the First World War, as can be seen by the style of the uniforms. By the time of the next poster, *bottom left,* the red coats are giving way to more sombre colours. In the final wartime example, *bottom right,* the message is far more explicit.

Above: Smiles all the way in Parliamentary Recruiting Committee poster No. 118.

Below: Recruiting posters were customised to suit local drives throughout the country. This one calls upon the men of Cambridgeshire and Suffolk to 'Obey the Call of Duty' by joining the Regular and Territorial battalions. And to prove that size, or lack of it, was not an impediment, men of 5 feet 3 inches could join a special Bantam Battalion. This poster, printed in Bristol, states that 'Little Men have made History. PLUCK can make up for inches.' It might sound ridiculous now, but it should be remembered that as a consequence of their diets the poorer or lower classes tended to be appreciably shorter than the better-fed ruling class.

Opposite: PRC poster No. 35. 'There is still a place in the line for YOU.' As if they were likely to run out of spaces.

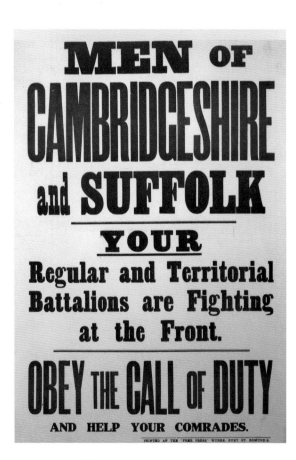

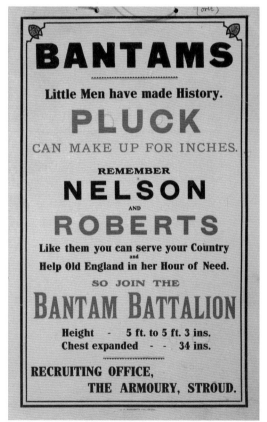

AN APPEAL TO YOU

"Give us a hand old man!"

'Give us a hand old man!' An example from the Central Council for Recruiting in Ireland – see also page 104.

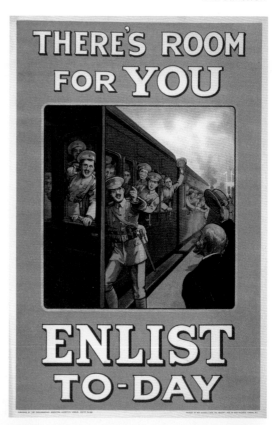

Pal Pressure

'Why not join the army?' These three posters are selling the army almost as a matter of a lifestyle choice for the duration. 'You will like it. Your pals will like it.' And, should you be in any doubt, there is a train full of them smiling and beckoning you to join in the fun.

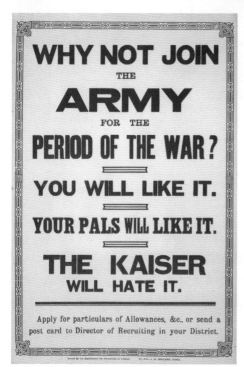

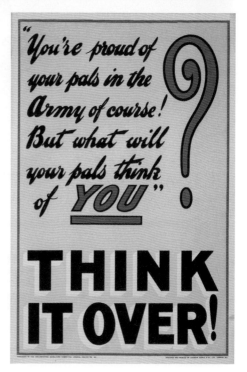

One of the earlier posters, No. 22, from the Parliamentary Recruiting Committee, featuring a smiling Tommy with his pipe. The quotation from General Sir Horace Smith-Dorrien states, 'The moment the order came to go forward, there were smiling faces everywhere.'

Poster No. 96. 'He's Happy & Satisfied. Are You?'

Above: It is an ordinary Tommy, not a figure of authority such as the king or even Lord Kitchener, who is inviting other young men at home to come and join him.

Opposite: 'Follow me!'

"This is not the time to play Games" *(Lord Roberts)*

RUGBY·UNION·FOOTBALLERS
are
DOING·THEIR·DUTY
over 90% have enlisted

"Every player who represented England in Rugby international matches last year has joined the colours."—Extract from *The Times*, November 30, 1914.

BRITISH ATHLETES!
Will you follow this
GLORIOUS EXAMPLE ?

ISSUED BY THE PUBLICITY DEPARTMENT, CENTRAL LONDON RECRUITING DEPOT, WHITEHALL, LONDON.   PRINTED BY JOHNSON, RIDDLE & CO., LTD., LONDON, S.E.

I
Playing the Game

At the start of the war there had been a push by the professional football clubs to carry on playing in order to keep people's spirits up. However, this backfired when public opinion openly turned against the football clubs. In 1914, Arthur Conan Doyle, the creator of Sherlock Holmes, made a direct appeal to footballers to volunteer for military service. 'If a footballer has strength of limb, let them serve and march in the field of battle.' Many footballers, and other sportsmen, heeded the call and a special Football Battalion was formed as a Pals Battalion within the Middlesex Regiment. During the war the regiment lost more than 1,000 men.

Right: Punch cartoon, October 1915. 'The Greater Game.'

Mr Punch (to Professional Association Player): 'No doubt you can make money in this field, my friend, but there's only one field today where you can get honour.' (The Council of the Football Association apparently proposes to carry out the full programme of the Cup Competition, just as if the country did not need the services of all its athletes for the serious business of War.)

Opposite: 'Rugby Union Footballers are doing their duty.' Poster published by the Publicity Department, Central London Recruiting Depot, Whitehall.

THE GREATER GAME.

Mr. Punch (*to Professional Association Player*). "NO DOUBT YOU CAN MAKE MONEY IN THIS FIELD, MY FRIEND, BUT THERE'S ONLY ONE FIELD TO-DAY WHERE YOU CAN GET HONOUR."

[The Council of the Football Association apparently proposes to carry out the full programme of the Cup Competition, just as if the country did not need the services of all its athletes for the serious business of War.]

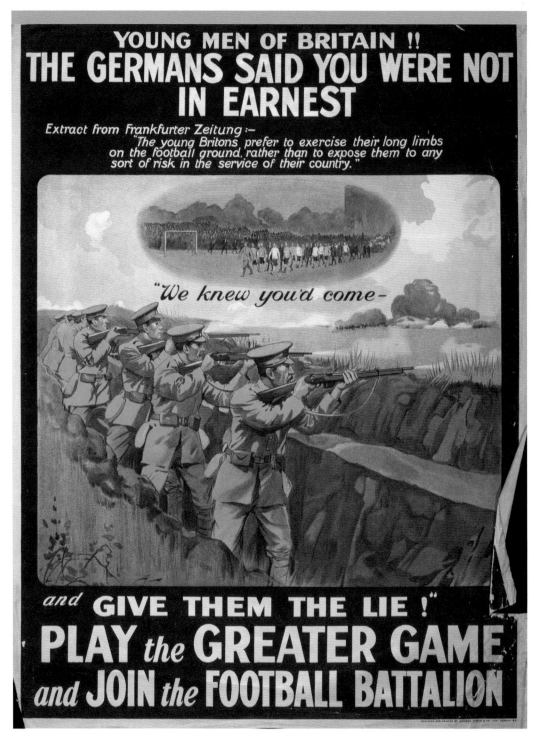

'Play the Greater Game and Join the Football Battalion.' If the Germans are saying that the young men of Britain prefer to 'exercise their long limbs on the football ground than expose them to any sort of risk in the service of their country,' then 'give them the lie!'

An unusually graphic poster image, reprinted from *The Weekly Dispatch* of 22 November 1914, and published by Associated Newspapers. The newspapers were far less likely to sugar-coat the realities of the war.

A GOOD RIDDANCE.

[The KING has done a popular act in abolishing the German titles held by members of His Majesty's family.]

Above: Punch cartoon showing King George V sweeping away his German family connections.

Opposite: Posters featuring the king were relatively few and far between, and in these examples the standard portrait makes only a cameo appearance. The example on the right was printed in Kingston, Jamaica. Kitchener had wanted all posters to end with 'God save the King!', but clearly this didn't happen.

2
For King and Country

King George V was the first cousin to Tsar Nicholas II of Russia and also to Kaiser Wilhelm II of Germany. The Kaiser was the eldest grandson of Queen Victoria, and it is said that his British relatives found him arrogant and obnoxious during his visits to England in the decades before the war. With the outbreak of hostilities in 1914, the public's loyalty to the king remained unquestioned, but these close family ties inevitably caused a discomfort among the royal family, and H. G. Wells went so far as to refer to them as Britain's 'alien and uninspiring court'. Even so, it wasn't until 1917 that the pressure of anti-German feelings persuaded the king to dissolve his ties with his German cousins. All German titles held by members of the royal family were relinquished and the House of Saxe-Coburg-Gotha became the more British-sounding House of Windsor.

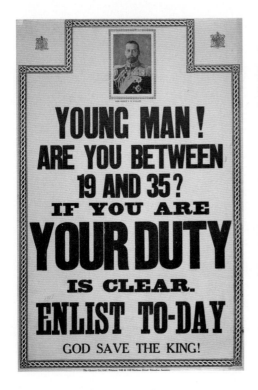
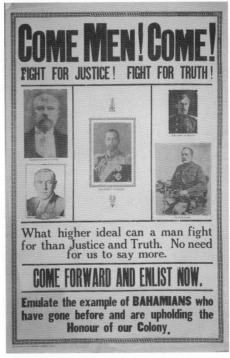

Linking the image of the king with country, or Empire, made it less about him as an individual and more about the greater concepts.

Opposite: Parliamentary Recruiting Committee poster No. 83.

Above: 'Our brave soldiers need your help.' PRC No. 10.

Below: Two map posters, Nos 126 and 23.

Rallying around the flag – a strong image from The Publicity Arts, London.

Three more examples of flag-based posters. Whether you call it the Union Jack or the Union Flag doesn't much matter according to the vexillologists. After much deliberation they have concluded that it could be called either. *Above left*: A very early poster printed very simply in two colours by letterpress using wooden blocks. *Above right*: An unusual appeal to the Jewish community. *Below*: A poster produced by the Publicity Department, Central Recruiting Office, Whitehall, featuring the flags of the Allies, including Russia and Japan. The United States did not join the war until 1917.

Four bold posters with the flag as the main motif. *Above:* An unnumbered poster published by the Parliamentary Recruiting Committee. *Below:* Two examples incorporating a standardised design. The one on the left is for the Royal Highlander Battalions in Canada, the other is the Parliamentary Recruiting Committee poster No. 5, published in November 1914. *Opposite:* The term 'Britishers' indicates that this poster was produced in the USA as an appeal to British men living there.

Could any symbol be more British than that of Saint George slaying the dragon? This is
Parliamentary Recruiting Committee poster No. 108...

… and this is the German take on the same theme. From a design by M. Lenz, it was published in 1917 and printed in Vienna, Austria. The slogan is for the sixth issue of war bonds. See also the British war bonds poster on page 162.

WHO FOLLOWS?

Britannia Rules

No one was spared. The ultimate British symbol was the figure of Britannia. Sometimes brandishing a Union Jack, she was summoned to recruit men aged between eighteen and sixty-one to enrol for the National Service Industrial Army. The National Service Department, later a ministry, was established to tackle the problem of maintaining a sufficient workforce for vital industries such as construction and agriculture. It was an entirely voluntary system.

Reproduced by special permission of the Proprietors of " PUNCH."
WHO FOLLOWS?
The Nation is Fighting for its Life
All Men should **ENROL for NATIONAL SERVICE**
FORMS FOR OFFER OF SERVICES CAN BE OBTAINED AT ALL POST OFFICES, NATIONAL SERVICE OFFICES, AND EMPLOYMENT EXCHANGES.
BRADBURY, AGNEW & CO., LTD., LONDON.

Left: 'Who follows?' The cartoon published in *Punch*, February 1917 (*top*), was copied for this poster. 'Forms for offer of services can be obtained at all Post Offices, National Service Offices and Employment Exchanges.'

Opposite: This poster features far more elaborate colour artwork by Septimus E. Scott.

REINFORCED CONCRETE.

JOHN BULL. "IF YOU NEED ASSURANCE, SIR, YOU MAY LIKE TO KNOW THAT YOU HAVE
THE LOYAL SUPPORT OF ALL DECENT PEOPLE IN THIS COUNTRY."

Punch cartoon, June 1915.

3
Kitchener's Army

Field Marshal Horatio Herbert Kitchener, the 1st Earl Kitchener, was a professional soldier who first won fame by winning the Battle of Omdurman in 1898 to secure the Sudan, after which he was given the title Lord Kitchener of Khartoum. As Chief of Staff in the Second Boer War (1900–1902) he played a vital part in Lord Roberts' campaign and he succeeded Roberts as Commander-in-Chief. In 1914, the Prime Minister, Herbert Asquith, appointed Kitchener as the Secretary of War. Recognising that this would be a long, drawn-out conflict, Kitchener organised the largest volunteer army that Britain had ever seen. The iconic image of Kitchener with pointed finger was produced by artist Alfred Leete as a cover illustration for the *London Opinion* magazine. In response to requests for copies it was also issued

Alfred Leete's classic design for *London Opinion*, and a photograph of Lord Kitchener.

'Who's absent?' John Bull in PRC poster No. 125. Printed in Newcastle-on-Tyne.

in postcard form. There is some disagreement concerning whether this design was actually used as a recruiting poster as such. On the one hand a report in *The Times* of 3 January 1915 describes its appearance at a recruiting rally in Trafalgar Square:

> Posters appealing to recruits are to be seen on every hoarding, in most windows, on omnibuses, tramcars and commercial vans. The great base of Nelson's Column is plastered with them. Their number and variety are remarkable. Everywhere Lord Kitchener points a monstrously big finger, exclaiming 'I Want You.'

This observation has been backed up by some historians, while others suggest that it was never used as a poster and has come to attention through the display of the original artwork at the Imperial War Museum. Either way, it has become an enduring image and possibly the most recognised of the First World War. It has gone on to

Lord Kitchener addresses the crowd at a recruitment rally. (J&C McCutcheon Collection)

inspire many other designs – most notably J. M. Flagg's poster of a pointing Uncle Sam – plus countless parodies over the years.

In addition to creating the so-called 'Kitchener's Army', the Secretary of War oversaw a massive expansion of munitions production at the start of the war. However, after being blamed by the newspapers for a shortage of shells, in the spring of 1915 he was stripped of his control over munitions and strategy and his public reputation was severely dented. On 5 June 1916 Lord Kitchener sailed to Scapa Flow where he boarded the warship HMS *Hampshire* for a diplomatic mission to Russia. Later that evening the *Hampshire* was caught in appalling weather en route to the Russian port Arkhangelsk, and while off the Orkney Islands the ship struck a mine laid by the German submarine U-75. Kitchener, his staff, and 643 out of 655 crew were drowned.

Above: Lord Kitchener in a solemn mood and without a pointing finger. The Kitchener 'I want you' poster was the direct inspiration for J. M. Flagg's Uncle Sam version produced for the US Army.

Opposite: Lord Roberts was a national hero whose image required no identification on this PRC poster, No. 20. Roberts had served in India during the rebellion, and led British forces to victory in the Second Boer War. He died of pneumonia in November 1914 after visiting Indian troops.

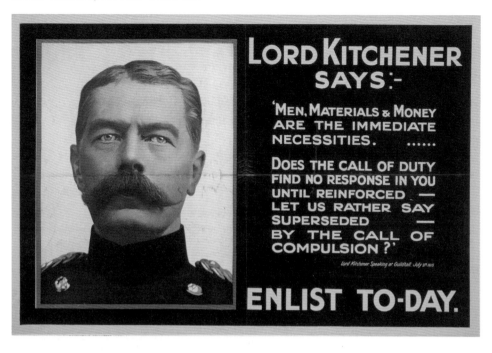

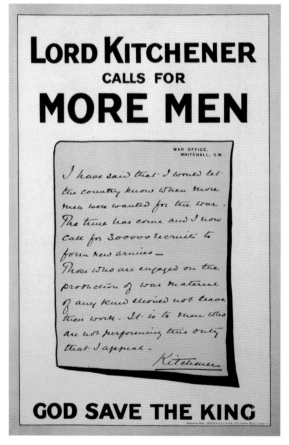

Above: Published in 1915, PRC poster No. 113.

Left: A message from Lord Kitchener. 'I have said that I would let the country know when more men were needed for the war. The time has come and I now call for 300,000 recruits to form new armies. Those who are engaged on the production of war material of any kind should not leave their work. It is to men who are not performing this duty that I appeal.'

Opposite: In this Canadian poster featuring Lord Kitchener his gaze is not fixed on the observer and, consequently, it loses much of its impact.

This beckoning recruiting sergeant is more likely to scare the recruits away.

AN APPEAL TO YOU

A far more friendly appeal on PRC poster No. 88.

THE VETERAN'S FAREWELL.

"Good Bye, my lad,
I only wish I were young enough
to go with you!"

ENLIST NOW!

The Veteran's Farewell

An unsophisticated approach perhaps, 'The Veteran's Farwell' conveyed a sense of continuing with tradition by taking up the fight for king, country and Empire. The nineteenth century had been littered with a string of conflicts, expeditions and campaigns in various parts of the Empire, including the two Boer Wars, and also the Anglo-Zulu War (1879). By 1914 only twelve years had passed since Britain had won the Second Anglo-Boer War against the Afrikaans-speaking settlers of the independent Boer republics in southern Africa. At the start of the First World War there was a genuine sense that this would be another short-lived conflict, one that could be handled by the professional army. Many of the newspapers and magazines published cartoons repeating this theme of the old generation passing on the baton to the new.

Opposite: In Frank Dadd's 1914 painting the red-coated veteran shakes the hand of the young man departing to fight. This is PRC poster No. 63, and the earlier monochrome version, No. 24, is shown *top right*.

Right: A similar theme enacted at the railway station, 'A Chip off the Old Block', is by Lawson Wood and is also dated 1914. PRC No. 18.

The bugle call sounds out 'Fall In'. This unnumbered poster printed in London reflects a heavy hand on the artist's part and is most probably a reworking of the design shown opposite.

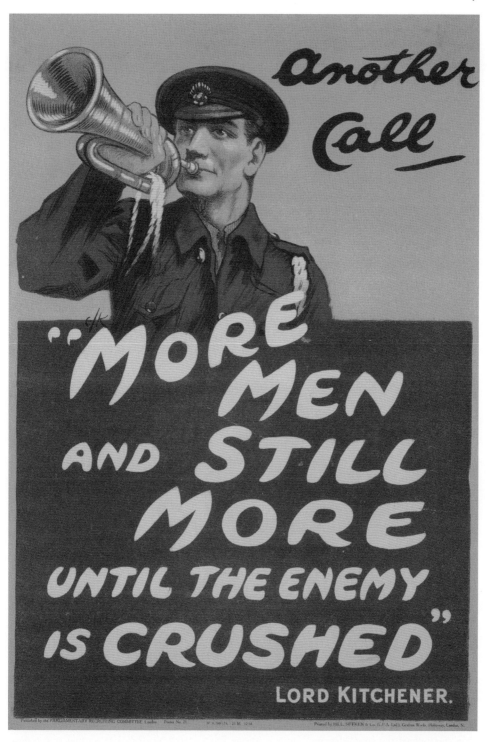

PRC poster No. 21, 'Another Call', with Lord Kitchener appealing for 'More men and still more until the enemy is crushed.'

'Boys come over here – you're wanted' and 'Boys! Come along – you're wanted' are obviously two versions of the same design. The top one is PRC poster No. 82. The simple two-colour version is PRC No. 80. Both posters were printed by David Allen & Sons of Harrow, Middlesex. No. 80 is a clearer design, although the soldier appears to be about to doff his hat rather than scan the horizon for reinforcements.

The numbers are truly staggering. 'Wanted 500,000 men.' A *Punch* illustration from September 1914 is used as a poster.

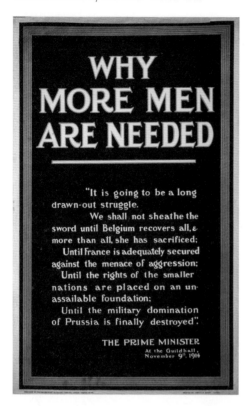

'Why more men are needed.' Forget any prospect of the fighting being over by Christmas, in November 1914 the Prime Minister is explaining that it will be 'a long drawn-out struggle'.

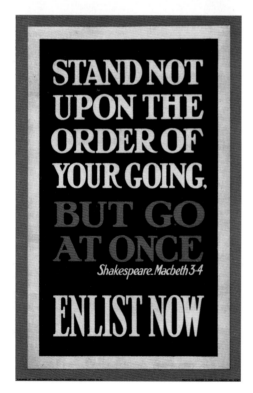

Poster quoting lines from *Macbeth*.

'An enquiry from the Front – When are the other boys coming?' and 'make us as proud of you ...' They were doing their bit, and now it was your turn.

"BE HONEST WITH YOURSELF. BE CERTAIN THAT YOUR SO-CALLED REASON IS NOT A SELFISH EXCUSE"

LORD KITCHENER

ENLIST TO-DAY

PUBLISHED BY THE PARLIAMENTARY RECRUITING COMMITTEE, LONDON. POSTER NO 127.   PRINTED BY BEHROSE & SONS LTD LONDON & DERBY. W 5768/578

If pride doesn't do the trick, then personal feelings of guilt – later to be reinforced by public and family pressure – might prove more persuasive.

Opposite: This is a bold design with effective block colour and a message from Lord Kitchener. 'Be honest with yourself. Be certain that your so-called reason is not an excuse.' PRC No. 127.

Right: 'There are three types of men.' PRC No. 93 puts the question into the mind of the viewer to engender a response.

Below: Simple black-and-white treatment for an earlier poster, PRC No. 38, but it is less subtle as the message to 'Think!' is in the form of an appeal rather than being thought provoking. A similar style of design is shown on page 93.

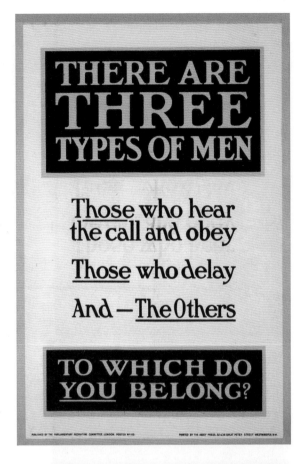

'Are YOU in this? 'A design by Lord Baden-Powell. Known for founding the Boy Scout movement, Baden-Powell had a distinguished military career and served in India and Africa. He is renowned for holding Mafeking during the Boer War. He was also an enthusiastic and capable artist and designed several theatre posters before the war. PRC No. 112 appears to be his only war poster, and although it might not be great art, it is workmanlike. Note the Boy Scout passing ammo up to the soldier.

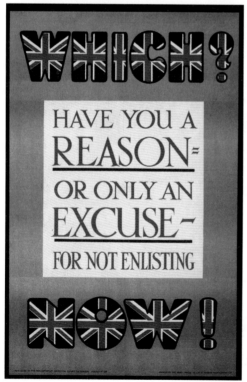

Left: A similar theme, if somewhat clumsily executed. PRC No. 128.

Opposite: Another straightforward question. PRC No. 65.

WHY AREN'T **YOU** IN KHAKI? YOU'LL BE WANTED. ENLIST AT ONCE.

Opposite: It's back to a very young-looking Boy Scout for PRC No. 121. This design is interesting because of the wall of recruiting posters in the background.

This page: Three fairly unremarkable posters with simple typographic appeals. 'Britain's Battle for Freedom' is PRC No. 44. The other two appear unnumbered and will have been produced using standard printer's wooden blocks.

IF THE
CAP FITS
YOU

JOIN
THE ARMY
TO-DAY.

'If the Cap fits...' At least the poster on the opposite page, PRC No. 53, has a certain appeal in its simplicity, but this later poster, No. 130, is just flabby and ineffective. It lacks impact and urgency and the image of a uniform hanging on the wall fails to capture the eye or the emotions.

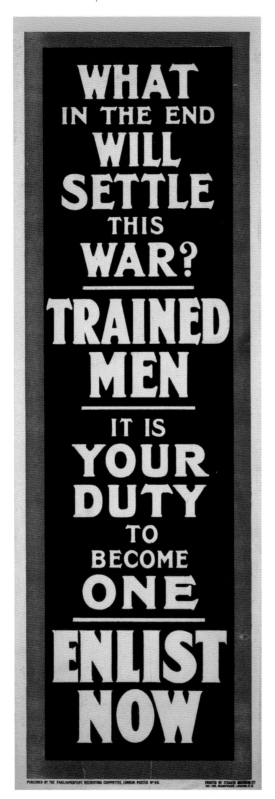

PUBLISHED BY THE PARLIAMENTARY RECRUITING COMMITTEE, LONDON POSTER Nº 66.   PRINTED BY STRAKER BROTHERS Cº

Two recruiting posters proclaiming the obvious merits of trained men. However, they are united by the common question, 'What in the end will settle this war?' It was a recurring theme that just one more push, one more injection of men, would tip the balance.

Left: PRC poster No. 66.

Opposite: A pleasing design for this early poster, PRC No. 34.

What in the end will settle this war?

TRAINED MEN

It is

YOUR DUTY

to become one

PUBLISHED BY THE PARLIAMENTARY RECRUITING COMMITTEE, LONDON.—POSTER No. 24.   PRINTED BY JAS. TRUSCOTT & SON, LTD., SUFFOLK LANE, LONDON, E.C.

Here the emphasis is on strength to appeal to a young man.

'Britain's strong arm and YOURS will carry us through.' PRC poster No. 28.

A curious metaphor implying that a final push is all that is needed to tip the red ball of victory over the top. Note how the German soldiers are faltering and the ball looks ready to roll down upon them. This is an unnumbered poster printed in Dublin.

More strong-arm tactics, in landscape formats.

Top: 'Lend your strong right arm for your country' is PRC No. 26. It is unusual in being a cut-out shape.

Middle: A straightforward typographic design on poster No. 48.

Bottom: 'Take up the Sword of Justice' is derived from the *Lusitania* poster shown on page 103. This is PRC No. 123.

It might not have been over by Christmas, but 1915 would bring victory, surely?

THE
NEW MILITARY SERVICE BILL
NEED NOT APPLY TO YOU IF YOU
ENLIST NOW
UNDER THE GROUP SYSTEM

MILLIONS of your Fellow Countrymen have volunteered their services

PLAY YOUR PART IN THIS
GREAT WORLD BATTLE
FOR FREEDOM
and let the State decide what that part shall be.

GROUP SYSTEM.

Enlistment in Groups will RE-OPEN ON MONDAY, January 10th, 1916, and proceed until further notice.

All Men between 18 and 41, both single and married, who have not yet attested should do so AT ONCE at the nearest Recruiting Office.

THE MONTH'S NOTICE TO MEN WHOSE GROUPS HAVE BEEN CALLED UP WILL COMMENCE FROM THE DATE OF THEIR ATTESTATION.

Above: Two typographic posters urging men to enlist under the group system by which they could stay together in the Army. This not only encouraged groups to enlist or attest at one go, but was also encouraged to create battalions that were more closely knit in battle.

Below: 'Wake up England – Complete the second half million.' The need for men was insatiable and by the end of the war in 1918 almost one in four of the adult male population in Britain – 5 million men – had joined up.

G. R.

"Wake up England"
Complete the Second Half-million

SINGLE MEN

Hundreds of Thousands of married men have left their homes to fight for **KING & COUNTRY**

SHOW YOUR APPRECIATION

BY FOLLOWING THEIR NOBLE EXAMPLE

PUBLISHED BY THE PARLIAMENTARY RECRUITING COMMITTEE, LONDON. POSTER Nº 120.   PRINTED BY THE ABBEY PRESS 32 & 34 ST PETER ST WESTMINSTER, S.W. W8855 20M-8/15.

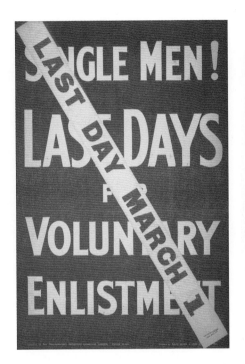

Single men were the natural target for the recruiters. Under the Derby Scheme, married men were given the assurance that single men would be called upon first. These posters were produced to encourage them to attest before the Military Service Bill came into effect in 1916.

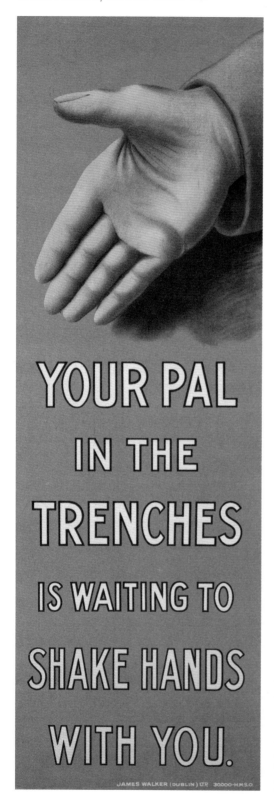

YOUR PAL IN THE TRENCHES IS WAITING TO SHAKE HANDS WITH YOU.

JAMES WALKER (DUBLIN) LTD 30000-H.M.S.O.

For obvious reasons there are no posters reflecting the reality of life in the trenches. These two convey the message that it is all about joining your pals.

Opposite: Once you get to the Front you can join their game of cards. This poster is printed in Dublin and issued by the Department of Recruiting for Ireland.

'Be ready!' A two-colour design featuring a silhouette with very subtle highlights. PRC No. 81.

Additional colour and more movement in this poster published by the Central Recruiting Committee, No. 2 Military Division, Toronto. See page 114.

Lads, you're wanted:
GO AND HELP.

The use of silhouettes negates the need to portray any sense of reality. The two examples on this page illustrate the reuse of a design. The long, thin version of 'Go and help', *above*, is PRC poster No. 78. The more conventionally shaped design, *below*, is PRC No. 73. Both are dated 1915.

Opposite: Less action, but a very interesting use of colour. 'Halt! Who goes there?' PRC poster No. 60, printed in London in 1915.

DON'T STAND LOOKING AT THIS
GO AND HELP!

'Mars Appeals to Vulcan', a *Daily Chronicle* war cartoon in poster form.

4
Poster Artists

Not all posters were produced by printers' jobbing artists and several notable artists provided artwork. Frank Brangwyn's designs are especially striking with their dark, brooding colours and strong visual treatment of the subject matter. Brangwyn was a Welshman born in Bruges in 1867, and he became a master of the lithographic print method, working directly on to limestone slabs. His style has been described as 'rugged' and some critics claim that his uncompromising realism portrayed the 'seamy side of war'. Either way there is no mistaking his work, and several examples are included in other sections of this book.

The reuse of a magazine cover in monochromatic form.

Through Darkness
to Light

**THE ONLY ROAD
FOR AN ENGLISHMAN**

Through Fighting
to Triumph

Left: 'The only road for an Englishman. Through Darkness to Light. Through Fighting to Triumph.' The work of another wartime lithographer, Gerald Spencer Pryse.

Below: A charity poster for the 1914 War Society, by Frank Brangwyn, and again, *opposite*, for the Sailors' and Soldiers' Tobacco Fund.

DO YOUR DUTY TO OUR BOYS AS
THEY ARE DOING THEIRS TO YOU!
THE 1914 WAR SOCIETY WANTS TO GIVE EVERY DISABLED MAN A FAIR
CHANCE OF HONOURABLE INDEPENDENCE IN HEALTHY RURAL SURROUNDINGS

DONATIONS
LARGE OR SMALL
BUT SEND NOW WHILE
YOU THINK OF IT
ADDRESS: 1914 WAR SOCIETY
28, DUKE ST, ST JAMES' W.

Designed by FRANK BRANGWYN, A.R.A.

SAILORS' & SOLDIERS' TOBACCO FUND

IT IS A SIGNIFICANT FACT THAT ALMOST
EVERY LETTER FROM THE FRONT CONTAINS
A REQUEST FOR "SOMETHING TO SMOKE".

Contributions gratefully received by
Hon. Sec., CENTRAL HOUSE, KINGSWAY, LONDON, W.C.

BRITISH NAVY AT WAR

ADMIRAL SIR DAVID BEATTY,
IN COMMAND OF THE GRAND FLEET.

The British Navy at War: Battleships steaming out to sea.

ADMIRAL SIR JOHN JELLICOE,
THE FIRST SEA LORD.

The interior of a British submarine: the living-space, looking aft.

Guarding the sea routes: in a British destroyer on patrol.

Wintry weather in the North Sea: a snow-clad British battleship.

In one of Britain's ship-building yards: a great destroyer on the stocks.

The interior of a British Submarine: the foremost torpedo-tubes.

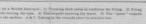

Torpedo-running practice on a British destroyer: (1) Training deck-tubes in readiness for firing. (2) Firing the torpedo. (3) The torpedo leaving the tube. (4) The torpedo entering the water. (5) The "spent" torpedo coming to the surface. (6 & 7) Taking in the torpedo after its practice run.

In a drifter on patrol: the gun in the bows ready for instant action.

Full steam ahead: a British battleship in a heavy sea.

Firing a salvo: the guns of a mighty British battleship in action.

Careless of wind and wave: a British battleship shipping a small sea.

Geo. Pulman & Sons Ltd., Thayer St., London, W.1.

1.

5
The Royal Navy

The army wasn't the only fighting force in the recruitment business. In the period before the war both sides had been in an arms race in which the Kaiser attempted to build a fleet to outstrip that of the UK. He failed, and in 1914 the Royal Navy remained the most powerful in the world, with a fleet that included eighteen modern dreadnoughts with more under construction. The Navy's strength was deployed in the British Grand Fleet which faced the Germans' High Seas Fleet across the North

THE WATCHERS OF THE SEAS.

THE NAVY NEEDS BOYS AND MEN FROM 15 TO 40 YEARS OF AGE.

APPLY: 7, WHITEHALL PLACE, S.W.

A NORTH SEA CHANTEY.
(To the tune of "Tipperary.")
JACK. "IT'S A LONG, LONG WAIT FOR WILLIAM'S NAVY, BUT MY HEART'S RIGHT HERE."

Opposite: 'British Navy at War.' The Navy's battleships are flanked by portraits of its leaders, Admiral Sir David Beatty, in charge of the Grand Fleet, and Admiral Sir John Jellicoe, the First Sea Lord.

Above: 'Watchers of the Seas', and a remarkably similar image which was published in *Punch*. 'It's a long, long wait for William's Navy, but my heart's right here.'

ROYAL NAVAL DIVISION

HANDYMEN TO FIGHT ON LAND & SEA

1ST BRIGADE		2ND BRIGADE
BATTALIONS:		BATTALIONS:
"BENBOW"		"HOWE"
"COLLINGWOOD"		"HOOD"
"HAWKE"		"ANSON"
"DRAKE"		"NELSON"

RECRUITS WANTED   **RECRUITS WANTED**

VACANCIES FOR RECRUITS BETWEEN THE AGES OF 18 AND 38

CHEST MEASUREMENT, 34 in.   HEIGHT, 5 ft. 3½ in.

PAYMENT FROM 1/3 PER DAY. FAMILY ALLOWANCES.

Besides serving in the above Battalions and for the Transport and Engineer Sections attached,

MEN WANTED

who are suitable for training as Wireless Operators, Signalmen, and other Service with the Fleet.

Apply to the Recruiting Office, 112, STRAND, LONDON, W.C.

EYRE & SPOTTISWOODE, Ltd., His Majesty's Printers, LONDON.

Sea. The only major naval conflict was the Battle of Jutland in May 1916, and despite losses, the Royal Navy maintained its dominance of the North Sea. Having the upper hand, it was able to impose a blockade on Germany, closing off access to both the North Sea and the English Channel. The greatest threat, therefore, was from the U-boats attacking merchant shipping in the Atlantic waters. For much of the war this submarine campaign was governed by rules requiring merchant ships to be warned and evacuated before being attacked. This arrangement was abandoned temporarily in 1915 and unrestricted warfare was resumed again in 1917, giving rise to the prospect of Britain being starved into submission.

During the First World War the Royal Navy's losses included two dreadnoughts, three battle-cruisers, eleven battleships, twenty-five cruisers, fifty-four submarines and sixty-four destroyers. In all, almost 35,000 men were killed and another 4,510 wounded.

For the sinking of the *Lusitania*, see page 99.

Opposite: Recruitment poster for the Royal Naval Division. 'Handymen to Fight on Land & Sea.' As it states, recruits had to be between the ages of eighteen and thirty-eight, with a chest measurement of 34 inches and a minimum height of 5 feet 3½ inches.

Above left: 'This is the only fashion for men for 1915.' A display outside the recruiting office on The Strand, complete with sailor. The lower poster featuring HMS *Victory* is shown overleaf.

Above right: 'Germany's Battle Cry is "Germany over All". And her navy drinks to "The Day" when she hopes to smash Britain's Fleet.' PRC poster No. 39, published in 1915.

*England Expects_*

and
England must not_and will not be disappointed.

RECRUITS WANTED
FOR THE
ROYAL NAVAL DIVISION
To serve during the Period of the War

AGE 18 TO 38 - MEAN CHEST MEASUREMENT 34 inches
HEIGHT 5 ft. 3½ inches.

There are NO EXPENSES incurred in joining FREE KITS and FOOD being provided.

Men are paid at the Service Rate of 1/3 per day - Separation allowances are made to the families of Married Men.

Apply to :-
THE ROYAL NAVAL DIVISION.
Recruiting Office : 112 THE STRAND, LONDON, W.C.

ANDREW REID & CO. L^TD. 50 GREY STREET NEWCASTLE-ON-TYNE.

1805 "ENGLAND EXPECTS" 1915

ARE YOU DOING YOUR DUTY TO-DAY ?

PUBLISHED BY THE PARLIAMENTARY RECRUITING COMMITTEE, LONDON. POSTER Nº 101.

PRINTED BY SPARGEANT BROS. LTD., LONDON & ABERGAVENNY. DESIGN COPYRIGHT.

Opposite: 'England Expects.' Nelson and his historic signal hoisted just before the Battle of Trafalgar in 1805 were obvious candidates for the recruiting posters. 'England must not and will not be disappointed', reassures this poster for recruits to the Royal Naval Division.

Above: This poster was issued by the Parliamentary Recruiting Committee and uses Nelson's message, although it is not specifically recruiting for the Royal Navy. PRC poster No. 101.

A very distinctive style for this poster, 'The Navy Wants Men'. The sailors in the crow's nest are very relaxed and look as if they are on holiday. Published by the Admiralty Recruiting Department.

'Royal Naval Division at Work & Play.' Not much evidence of the play aspect.

'Join the Royal Marines – Help to man the guns of the Fleet.' It all sounds a little too polite, an invitation for help, and note the sailor who has turned to smile at the observer.

Interesting example of recycling a poster design.

Top: 'Remember England Expects' again, this time for the Navy, with a space for recruiting office details to be added. Printed in Leeds.

Bottom: The same design, reused for the Royal Naval Canadian Volunteer Overseas Division, and printed in Canada.

6

Barbarous Acts

Atrocities and acts of cruelty have been a constant in the vocabulary of the propagandists. What better way to demonise your enemy. The 'Scrap of Paper' in the poster, *opposite*, refers to the 1839 treaty signed by both Britain and Germany to guarantee the independence and neutrality of Belgium. PRC No. 15.

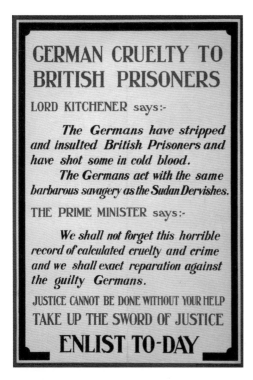

Above left: 'German Cruelty to British Prisoners.' Lord Kitchener and the Prime Minister lend weight to the claims of 'barbarous savagery'. Another commonly stated accusation was that the Germans were 'Baby Killers'. It should be noted that the Third Geneva Convention – the part that relates to the treatment of prisoners of war – was not adopted until 1929. In essence, it stated that prisoners of war were the responsibility of the state, not the persons who capture them, and that torture may not be used against them. Prisoners must be treated humanely and their medical needs met.

Above right: 'The barbarian is almost at your gates. He violates, plunders, murders. Don't let him get a footing on British soil.'

THE "SCRAP OF PAPER"

These are the signatures and seals of the representatives of the Six Powers to the "Scrap of Paper"——the Treaty signed in 1839 guaranteeing the independence and neutrality of Belgium.

"Palmerston" signed for Britain, "Bülow" for Prussia.

The Germans have broken their pledged word and devastated Belgium. Help to keep your Country's honour bright by restoring Belgium her liberty.

ENLIST TO-DAY

PUBLISHED BY THE PARLIAMENTARY RECRUITING COMMITTEE, LONDON.—POSTER NO. 18—W.4500—6000—4/15

Some posters raised the political aspects of the war. 'Remember Belgium' was a common slogan in the earlier stages. PRC poster No. 19, printed in Leeds.

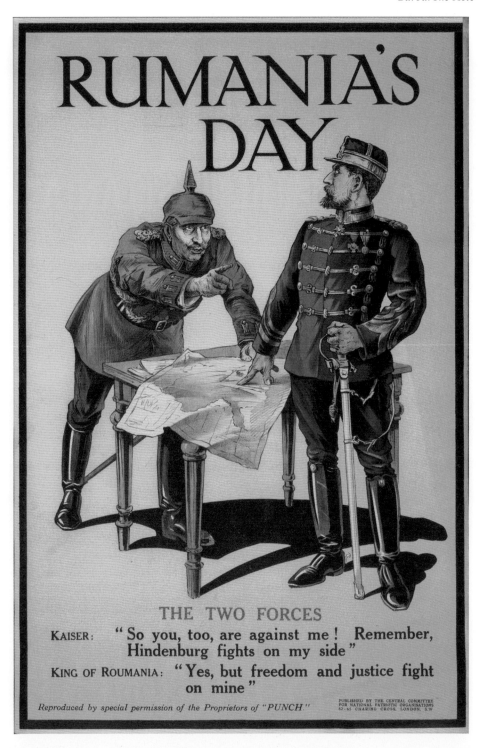

'Rumania's Day.' As seen elsewhere, the newspaper and magazine cartoonists were more eloquent in their analysis. Published by the Central Committee for National Patriotic Organisations.

7
The *Lusitania*

Launched in 1904, Cunard's RMS *Lusitania* was the largest ship in the world at the time. As a passenger liner her transatlantic crossings continued after the outbreak of war, protected by the Cruiser Rules, which had been established by various international agreements and clearly stated that passenger ships may not be sunk, and that crews of merchant ships must be placed in safety before their ship may be sunk. By the spring of 1915, submarine warfare in the Atlantic had intensified and the German Embassy in Washington placed newspaper advertisements warning people not to sail on the *Lusitania*. On 1 May 1915 she left New York, bound for Liverpool. Six days later, on the afternoon of 7 May, the *Lusitania* was 11 miles off the Irish coast when she was struck by a single torpedo fired from the submarine U-20. Moments later a second explosion reverberated through the hull and the ship

A contemporary illustration depicting the dreadful moment when the torpedo struck RMS *Lusitania*, 7 April 1915.

quickly began to list to starboard, hindering the launching of lifeboats. Of the 1,959 passengers and crew on board the *Lusitania*, 1,195 lost their lives. Most of them British or Canadian.

The sinking of the *Lusitania* had been a blatant breach of the international Cruiser Rules, although the Germans claimed that the ship was a legitimate target as a naval vessel because she was openly carrying munitions – the 'contraband of war' – in her cargo. The incident caused a storm of protest, not least because of the indiscriminate death of women and children. The Americans were especially outraged by the loss of 128 of its citizens and a contemporary cartoon, published by *Punch* five days after the sinking, depicts the figure of Britannia addressing America (see above).

> In silence you have looked on felon blows,
>   On butcher's work of which the waste lands reek;
> Now, in God's name, from Whom your greatness flows,
>   Sister, will you not speak.

'Remember *Lusitania*.' A British recruiting officer in Bermondsey refers to a poster featuring the ocean liner. (J&C McCutcheon Collection)

The sinking of the *Lusitania* also coloured public opinion on this side of the Atlantic and the event became a rallying point for the recruiting campaign. Under the banner 'Remember the *Lusitania*', one British poster remonstrated against 'this devil's work':

> This appalling crime was contrary to international law and the conventions of all civilised nations, and we therefore charge the officers of the said submarine, the Emperor and Government of Germany, under whose orders they acted, with the crime of wilful and wholesale murder before the tribunal of the civilised world. It is your duty to take up the sword of justice.

The Americans were shocked by the sinking, and President Woodrow Wilson warned Germany not to attack neutral US ships. For a while they acquiesced. Then, at the beginning of 1917, Germany decided to resume all-out submarine attacks on all commercial vessels heading to the United Kingdom. Once the submarines began sinking American ships, Woodrow Wilson called upon Congress for a 'war to end all wars'. The USA abandoned its neutrality and entered the First World War on 6 April 1917.

REMEMBER THE
LUSITANIA

THE JURY'S VERDICT SAYS:
"We find that the said deceased died from their prolonged immersion and exhaustion in the sea eight miles south south-west of the Old Head of Kinsale on Friday, May 7th, 1915, owing to the sinking of the R.M.S. Lusitania by a torpedo fired without warning from a German submarine."

"That this appalling crime was contrary to international law and the conventions of all civilized nations, and we therefore charge the officers of the said submarine, the Emperor and Government of Germany, under whose orders they acted, with the crime of wilful and wholesale murder before the tribunal of the civilized world."

IT IS **YOUR DUTY** TO **TAKE UP THE SWORD OF JUSTICE**
TO AVENGE THIS DEVIL'S WORK.

ENLIST TO-DAY

PUBLISHED BY THE PARLIAMENTARY RECRUITING COMMITTEE LONDON. POSTER No 87   PRINTED BY DAVID ALLEN & SONS LD. HARROW MIDDLESEX.

'Remember *Lusitania* – Enlist Today.'

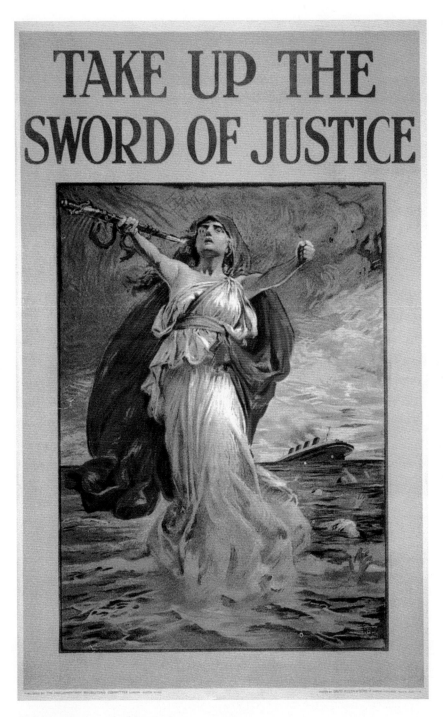

'Take up the sword of Justice.'

8

Ireland in the War

As a part of the United Kingdom at the outbreak of the war, Ireland inevitably became embroiled in the fighting. Many people in Ireland supported the war and, initially at least, they backed the British war effort. But the political situation in

Opposite: In general the Irish recruitment posters were far less strident than those produced by the PRC in London. 'I'll go too!' Published by the General Council for the Organisation of Recruiting in Ireland.

Above left: 'Ireland's War Map.' The Irish regiments acquitted themselves well in the major campaigns of the war. In addition to the home-grown regiments, many Irishmen were able to join Irish regiments of the regular British Army based in England, Scotland and Wales.

Above right: This poster extols every Irishman to do their duty to their country, but no mention of the king is included of course.

Ireland remained complex and highly volatile. The Third Home Rule Act, which had received Royal Assent on September 1914, was suspended for the duration of the war.

Over 200,000 Irishmen served in the British forces during the war, including 130,000 recruits, although the rate of recruitment fell sharply following the Easter Rising of 1916. Conscription was proposed but never instigated by the authorities, who were faced with the prospect of a mass civil disobedience. The final casualty figures among the Irish servicemen vary according to different sources, but it is generally accepted that the figure is somewhere between 30,000 and 35,000 men.

At the end of the war Sinn Fein won the Irish General Election of 1918, and this led to the Irish Declaration of Independence from the British and the subsequent fight for its freedom.

Three more Irish recruiting posters:

Above left: 'For the glory of Ireland, will you go or must I?' An unusually underhand message.

Above right: A very rare use of religious imagery in a recruiting poster.

Opposite: 'The call to arms. Irishmen don't you hear it?' Bagpipes, an Irish hound, flags, soldiers marching and a sunrise over the Emerald Isle, all on the one poster.

9

Scotland in the War

Although the Scots accounted for only 10 per cent of the population, they accounted for 15 per cent of the manpower within Britain's forces. This is due, in part, to the poverty in many of Scotland's urban centres – rich pickings for the British recruiting officers – together with the promise of a government stipend for life to take care of their dependants. Scotland played a vital role in the conflict, providing men, ships and food, but the Scots paid a high price, and across the ten Scottish regiments it is estimated that around 100,000 men were lost out of the 690,000 who went to fight.

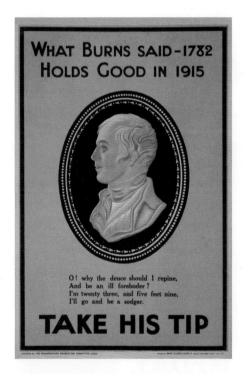

Opposite: 'A wee "scrap" o' paper" is Britain's bond.' PRC poster No. 17.

Above: Robbie Burns, Scotland's favourite son, lends his voice to the call for men to enlist. Poster published by the PRC in 1915. And a Fougasse cartoon from *Punch*, 'Scotland for ever!'

'Line up, boys!' PRC poster No. 54.

A Canadian recruiting poster for the 91st Highlanders.

10

Wales in the War

The Welsh Regiment had been formed in 1881, and during the First World War it raised thirty-four Regular, Territorial, Reserve and Service battalions. These fought at a variety of locations including Gallipoli, Salonika, Egypt and Palestine as well as on the Western Front. Members of the regiment won three VCs.

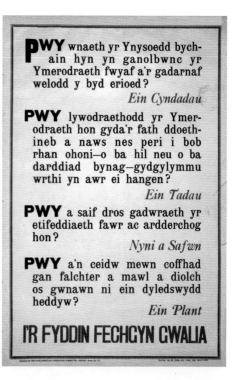

Above: One poster in two languages. Both issued by the PRC.

Opposite: Poster by the Welsh artist Frank Brangwyn, announcing a grand matinee on St David's Day in aid of the National Fund for Welsh Troops.

CANADA!

YPRES: APRIL 22—24, 1915.

11

Rallying the Empire

The First World War came at a time when the sun never set on the British Empire and Britain's declaration of war on Germany and her allies also committed the colonies and dominions to provide military, financial and material support. Over 2.5 million men served in the armies of the Dominions and played a significant part in the military campaigns, in particular the Canadian troops at Vimy Ridge, and both the Australians and New Zealanders during the Gallipoli campaign against the Ottoman Empire in the Dardanelles in Turkey.

The death tolls of the major participating countries read with shocking inevitability. India tops the table with 74,000 men lost, then comes Canada with nearly 65,000, Australia with almost 62,000, New Zealand 18,000 and South Africa with around 9,500.

As it did with so many aspects of life, the First World War brought great change and many commentators regard it as a turning point in the fate of the Empire nations, igniting a spark that engendered a greater sense of independent identities. The war had begun with four great empires, but it ended with only one intact. Ironically, the end of the war actually saw the British Empire reach its greatest extent as former Ottoman and Germany colonies were absorbed, resulting in the addition of 1,800,000 square miles of new territory, plus some 13 million new subjects, under the terms of the 1919 Treaty of Versailles.

Opposite: Punch cartoon marking the Canadian contribution at Ypres. Published 5 May 1915.

Opposite: 'Britishers you're needed.' At the start of the war the call went out to all British expats to return to fight for the motherland. Published by the British & Canadian Recruiting Mission.

Right: The strength of Frank Brangwyn's poster is a stark image and a call to the Empire.

WAR
TO ARMS CITIZENS OF THE EMPIRE!!

WE WILL UPHOLD THE PRICELESS GEM OF LIBERTY
"For Gold the Merchant Ploughs the Main
The Farmer tills the Manor
But Glory is the Soldier's Prize
The Soldier's Wealth is Honour"

SHALL WE HELP TO CRUSH TYRANNY?
APPLY AT RECRUITING STATION

'Shall we help to crush tyranny?' The discreet maple leaves reveal this poster's Canadian origins. It was printed in Montreal.

'The Empire Needs Men!' The Old Lion of Britain helped by the young lions of the Empire nations. PRC poster No. 58.

Poster for the Overseas Battalion.

Opposite: 'We go next!' Irish Canadian Rangers for the Overseas Battalion.

Right: 'Australia's Imperishable Record.' A commendation for the Aussies and Kiwis from General Sir Ian Hamilton, 1915. Printed in Sydney. Note the Union Jacks even though Australia had its own national flag since 1901.

'The Kilties are Here!' British Recruiting Week in the USA.

ROYAL PROCLAMATION
YOU ARE ASKED
TO REDUCE YOUR
CONSUMPTION OF
BREAD BY $\frac{1}{4}$

THE PRICE OF VICTORY.

"WELL, OLD GIRL, IF WE CAN'T DO THAT MUCH, WE DON'T DESERVE TO WIN."

12

The Home Front

The war of 1914–18 was the first 'total war' in which every man, woman and child at home was directly affected in their daily lives. This meant hardships for most of the civilian population in terms of food shortages, changes to their work and, ultimately, the risk of being injured or even killed in enemy raids. Putting aside the recruitment drive and the terrible loss of life in the trenches – and just about everyone was touched by that – the posters on the newly termed 'Home Front' had the dual purpose of providing information to the public while also ensuring that they behaved appropriately and did their bit.

For the British the U-boat attacks on merchant shipping caused shortages of food and led to the first nationwide food restrictions. These were fairly tentative at first and in 1916 the Ministry of Food was tasked with making the nation more self-sufficient with measures to improve food distribution. An additional 3 million acres of land was taken over for farming, much of it worked by the Woman's Land Army – see page 139 for more on the changing role of women.

Basics such as flour, butter, eggs, milk and meat remained in short supply and the public was urged to avoid all waste and, in particular, to save bread as this was the staple diet of the poorer classes. Food rationing was introduced in early 1918, but the cartoonists and the signs that appeared above the store fronts spelt out the issue of inequality. 'If you are rich, defeat for Great Britain is at your command', stated one notice. 'In honour bound, do you live within the national scale of rations?' Wartime recipe books suggested alternatives to traditional ingredients such as the use of potatoes in place of flour, and their pages offered new culinary delights such as ox brain fritters, fish custard and trench pudding. In the words of one recipe book author, 'If you cannot have the best, make the best of what you have.'

Opposite: Punch cartoon, published in May 1917.

BAD FORM IN DRESS.

The National Organizing Committee for War Savings appeals against extravagance in women's dress.

Many women have already recognized that elaboration and variety in dress are bad form in the present crisis, but there is still a large section of the community, both amongst the rich and amongst the less well-to-do, who appear to make little or no difference in their habits.

New clothes should only be bought when absolutely necessary, and these should be durable and suitable for all occasions. Luxurious forms, for example, of hats, boots, shoes, stockings, gloves, and veils should be avoided.

It is essential, not only that money should be saved, but that labour employed in the clothing trades should be set free.

TO DRESS EXTRAVAGANTLY IN WAR TIME IS WORSE THAN BAD FORM IT IS UNPATRIOTIC

WAR ECONOMY.

Lady Sybil de Vere. "Do look at those extraordinary people. Their clothes are quite new!"
Sir Hugo. "Rotten bad form!"

The National Committee for War Savings made appeals against extravagance in women's dress. 'To dress extravagantly in wartime is worse than bad form, it is unpatriotic.' The cartoon, *above*, is from November 1915 and reveals the effects of the war economy on some. Reinforcing peer pressure was part of the wider propaganda campaign to influence the public's behaviour in a way that had never been seen before.

DON'T

1. Don't use a motor car or motor cycle for pleasure purposes.

2. Don't buy new clothes needlessly. Don't be ashamed of wearing old clothes in War time.

3. Don't keep more servants than you really need.

In this way you will save money for the War, set the right example, and free labour for more useful purposes.

Your Country will Appreciate Your Help.

'Don't' – three ways to aid the war effort. Reduce petrol consumption, don't buy new clothes and, of course, don't keep more servants than you really need. 'In this way you will save money for the War, set the right example, and free labour for more useful purposes.' The poster concludes in a thoroughly British way: 'Your country will appreciate your help.'

ARE YOU HELPING THE GERMANS?

You are helping the Germans
When you use a Motor Car for pleasure.
When you buy extravagant clothes.
When you employ more servants than you need.
When you waste coal, electric light or gas.
When you eat and drink more than is necessary to your health and efficiency.

SET THE RIGHT EXAMPLE, free labour for more useful purposes, save money and lend it to the Nation and so

HELP YOUR COUNTRY

This poster is more direct in showing that such excess of consumption could be helping the Germans. But the reference to servants doesn't sit easily with modern sensibilities.

ISSUED BY THE PUBLICITY DEPARTMENT, CENTRAL RECRUITING DEPOT, WHITEHALL, S.W.   ANDREW REID & CO., LTD., 50, GREY STREET, NEWCASTLE-ON-TYNE.

The Zeppelin Menace

At the outbreak of the war the German Army had six rigid-frame airships and the Navy had one. Universally known as Zeppelins, they were built by two rival companies, Zeppelin and Shutte-Lanz. Initially their role was seen as reconnaissance, especially for the German Navy, while the Army's experiments with the aerial bombardment of Liège and Antwerp had proved unpromising. Under the command of Peter Strasser, however, the Imperial Navy's aerial fleet began to grow and they patrolled the North Sea. Having demonstrated their range and a degree of reliability, Strasser and the admiralty urged the Kaiser to give permission for attacks on England. Reluctantly he agreed in January 1915, although he stipulated that the raids were to be on military targets and that London was to be excluded. The first successful raid took place on the night of 15/16 January 1915 when two Zeppelins targeting Humberside were diverted off course by strong winds and dropped their bombs on Great Yarmouth and the Sherringham area of Norfolk. Four people were killed and sixteen injured in the raid. The bombing of London's docks was authorised the following month but the first attempts were thwarted by the weather. On 31 May the LZ 38 made the first raid on London, dropping 120 bombs, which resulted in the deaths of seven people and injured thirty-five. The raids continued into 1916, but by then the British defences had been much improved and the use of incendiary bullets made the hydrogen-filled airships highly vulnerable, causing the Germans to respond by lightening their craft to enable them to fly at higher altitudes. On the night of 2/3 September 1916, Captain William Leefe Robinson became the first British pilot to shoot down a German airship encountered over Potters Bar. Although described as a Zeppelin, this was actually one of the Shutte-Lanz wooden-framed crafts.

In early 1917 the Gotha bomber aircraft began daylight attacks on London and the casualties were correspondingly much higher. The last of the Gotha raids took place on the night of 19 May 1918, with the forty-one aircraft suffering heavy losses. The final Zeppelin raid was on 5 August 1918, when four airships attacked targets in the Midlands. In total, fifty-one airship raids were carried out on England, resulting in 557 deaths and injuring another 1,358 people. Without doubt the raids had caused considerable alarm and they were a precursor to the more devastating strategic bombing of the Second World War.

Opposite: The Zeppelin raids brought a new terror to Londoners and provided a new ogre for the recruiting posters to exploit.

Another classic Frank Brangwyn poster, this one produced from a drawing for *The Daily Chronicle*. The claim of protection for their readers from the risks of bombardment or aeroplanes is interesting. It conjures up images of people holding the newspaper over their heads during a raid.

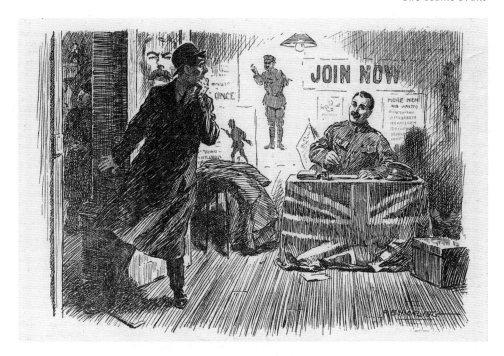

Above: Punch cartoon from November 1915. Entitled 'During a Zeppelin raid', the caption reads, 'Predicament of an unstarred man who has taken the first available cover.' Note the posters on the wall; the figure of the beckoning recruiting sergeant is on one – see page 48 – and there's the familiar face of Lord Kitchener.

Below: The Zeppelins were a gift to the cartoonists. This is a postcard poking fun at 'The Gasbag'.

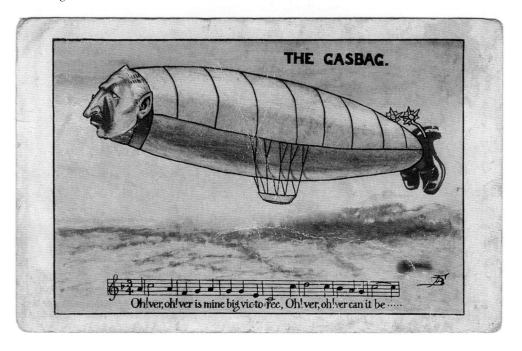

THE
SPORTSMAN BATTALION'S
RECRUIT
WHO WRECKED THE ZEPPELIN
and won the V.C.

By permission of F. M. Birkett and The "Daily Sketch."

FOLLOW HIS LEAD
AND JOIN THE
SPORTSMAN'S BATTALION

Apply E. CUNLIFFE-OWEN, Hotel Cecil, Strand, London,

W. STRAKER, Ltd., Printers, 13, Coventry Street, Piccadilly, W.

The Zeppelin factor: The Sportsman Battalion's recruit who felled a Zeppelin is featured in this poster on the opposite page.

Above: A Zeppelin-inspired enlistment poster, and an information poster helping the public to correctly identify German and British aircraft. Both airships and Gotha bombers were used in the air raids on England.

Below: A heart-rending image by the Dutch artist Louis Raemaekers. '… But Daddy, mother didn't do anything wrong!'

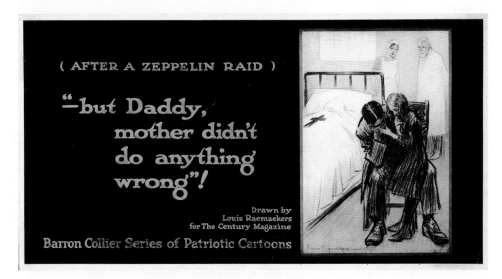

MEN OF BRITAIN !
WILL YOU STAND THIS ?

PHOTO. BY F. FOXTON, SCARBOROUGH.

Nº 2 *Wykeham Street,* SCARBOROUGH, *after the German bombardment on Decʳ 16th. It was the Home of a Working Man. Four People were killed in this House including the Wife, aged 58, and Two Children, the youngest aged 5.*

78 Women & Children were killed and 228 Women & Children were wounded by the German Raiders
ENLIST NOW

Scarborough

Zeppelins and aeroplanes were not the only means of striking the British mainland. On 16 December 1914 the German Imperial Navy launched an attack on the seaports of Scarborough, Hartlepool and Whitby in an attempt to draw out the British Royal Navy. Shells fired from the German ships killed 137 people and injured 592 more, including many civilians. This attack on civilians had an enormous effect on public opinion, making 'Remember Scarborough!' the new rallying call for the recruiting posters.

Opposite: 'Men of Britain will you stand this?' The poster spells out the result of a shell landing on No. 2 Wykeham Street in Scarborough. 'It was the home of a working man. Four people were killed in this house, including the wife, aged fifty-eight, and two children, the youngest aged five.' The image of the destruction tallies with the newspaper photographs of the time, and to tug at the heartstrings the poster artist has included the figure of a small girl carrying a baby. PRC poster No. 51.

Above: A blunt declaration that this atrocity only strengthened Britain's resolve to 'crush the German barbarians'. PRC poster No. 29, printed in London. Plus an illustrated poster featuring Britannia with the flames of Scarborough burning against the night sky. PRC No. 41.

Take the soldier out of the picture and this could be a travel poster. PRC No. 87, printed in Leeds.

A more graphic portrayal with the enemy forcing their way through the door. A poster printed in Dublin.

An interesting poster published by London Underground. Under the influence of Frank Pick, the Underground had developed a strong visual identity and a reputation for the quality of its posters. The caption at the top reads, 'The Underground Railways of London, knowing how many of their passengers are now engaged on important business in France and other parts of the world, send out this reminder of home.' Thanks are due to George Clausen RA for the drawing. At the bottom there are lines of verse by Samuel Rogers.

Left: An advertising poster from London Underground in dubious taste. 'Why bother about the Germans invading the country. Invade it yourself …' Published in 1915.

Opposite: Back to the realities of the war, this poster by F. Gregory Brown for war savings certificates shows the consequences for the British if the Germans were to invade.

13
Women at War

In the early stages of the war the women of Britain were regarded with little interest by the establishment. However, the authorities were happy enough to have them act as recruiting agents within the home. They were urged to pack their men off to war, to 'Say GO!' and wave them goodbye. It wasn't just their own men that they cajoled into enlisting either. The white feather movement sprung up with the purpose of publicly humiliating any man who looked, in their eyes, like a shirker, presenting them with a white feather as a mark of cowardice. Men in reserved occupations were not immune to their attentions and a badge scheme was introduced to identify and protect them.

Many women immersed themselves in countless good causes for the war effort, working voluntarily for various charities. But as the war progressed the role of women in society underwent enormous change, and while it is tempting to suggest that the war progressed the cause of the Suffragettes, it is generally recognised that it most probably held back what was only inevitable. Women were not expected to fight, of course, but they marched through London to demand the 'right to serve' in other ways, and as the available manpower on the Home Front began to dwindle while the need for increased production rocketed, it was recognised that women had to fill the gap. Women from all strata of society took on a range of tasks previously undertaken by men. They worked on the buses as 'clippies' and on the trains as porters, they drove ambulances, they worked on the land and, most importantly of all, they reported for work at the munitions factories in their droves. For many women it must have been an enormous transition going from their homes to the noise and bustle of the factories. It was difficult and dangerous work too, and handling the TNT used in the manufacturer of shells caused many to become sick with a form of jaundice; some even died.

Opposite: One of the best-known posters of the First World War. It clearly places women in a passive role, but as the war continued they came to play an increasingly active part in all aspects of life on the Home Front.

Next page: Mothers and wives bid farewell to their menfolk.

Above: 'Go. It's your duty lad.' All female members of the family, young and old, were encouraged to send their men to the fighting. PRC poster No. 109, printed in Harrow, Middlesex, in 1915.

Below: A Punch cartoon from 21 February 1917.

Instructor (to very nervous lady, who, with a view to war-work, is inquiring about tuition). "OF COURSE YOU WOULD BEGIN ON A LOW-POWERED CAR, AND THEN WE SHOULD TAKE YOU IN A 40—50, AND FINISH YOU OFF IN TRAFFIC."

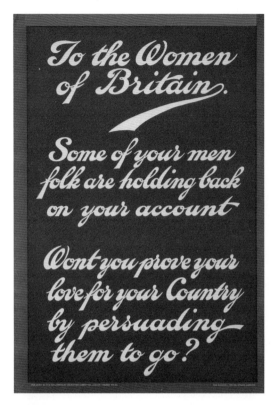

'To the Women of Britain. Some of your men folk are holding back on your account. Won't you prove your love for your Country ...' When even the members of their own families were persuading them to go, the pressure on the men must have been overwhelming.

This Irish poster is appealing to the men, implying the consequences for their 'women folk' if they don't take action. 'Have you any women-folk worth defending?'

Child (much impressed by martial emblems opposite). " MOTHER, IS THAT A SOLDIER? " *Mother.* "NO, DARLING." *Child.* "WHY NOT?"

Above: Punch cartoon,
published in December 1914.
    Child (much impressed by
martial emblems opposite):
'Mother is that a soldier?'
Mother: 'No, darling.' *Child:*
'Why not?'

Right: 'Let there not be a man or
a woman among us who, when
the war is over, will not then be
able to say: I was not idle.' The
words of the Prime Minister in
May 1915.

Let there not be a man
or a woman among us
who, when the war is
over, will not then be
able to say:

" I was not idle.

"I took such part as I
could in the greatest task
which, in all the storied
annals of our country, has
ever fallen to the lot of
Great Britain to achieve".

THE PRIME MINISTER.
May 4th 1915.

TO THE WOMEN OF BRITAIN.

1. You have read what the Germans have done in Belgium. Have you thought what they would do if they invaded this Country **?**

2. Do you realise that the safety of your home and children depends on our getting more men **NOW** **?**

3. Do you realise that the one word "GO" from you may send another man to fight for our King and Country **?**

4. When the War is over and someone asks your husband or your son what he did in the great War, is he to hang his head because you would not let him go **?**

WON'T YOU HELP AND SEND A MAN TO JOIN THE ARMY TO-DAY?

PUBLISHED BY THE PARLIAMENTARY RECRUITING COMMITTEE, LONDON.—POSTER NO. 65.   PRINTED BY BEMROSE & SONS LTD. LONDON AND DERBY

Another appeal to the women of Britain to send a man to join the army. This time implying that the women may be holding their husbands and sons back.

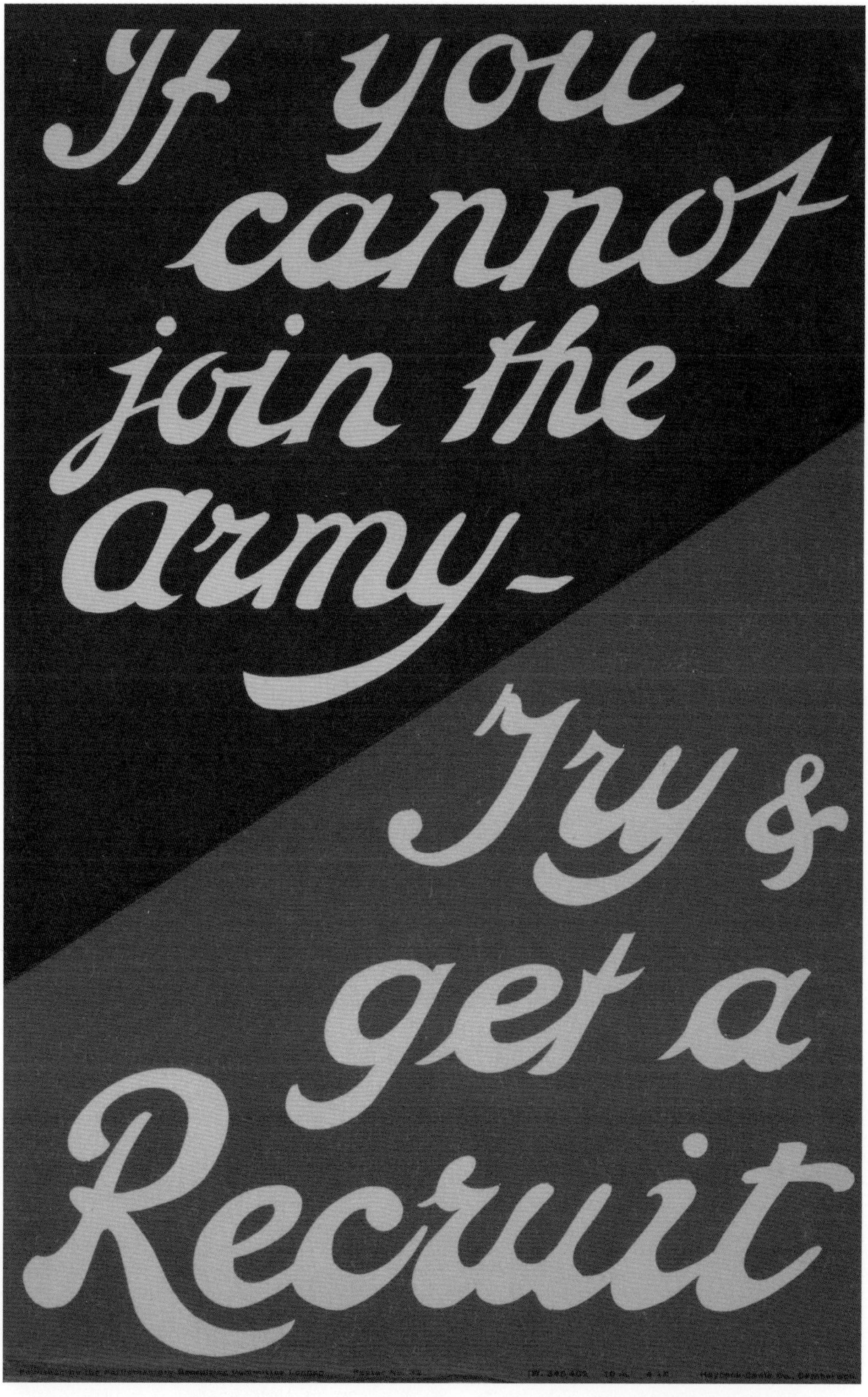

If you
cannot
join the
Army -

Try &
get a
Recruit

Above: Sidelined at first, women marched through London to demand the 'right to serve'. Lloyd George had actually recruited the help of the Suffragette Emmeline Pankhurst to organise the demonstration. (J&C McCutcheon Collection)

Below: The reality of working in a munitions factory. It could be difficult and, sometimes, highly dangerous work handling the chemicals for the shells. There was also the ever-present risk of an accident. (J&C McCutcheon Collection)

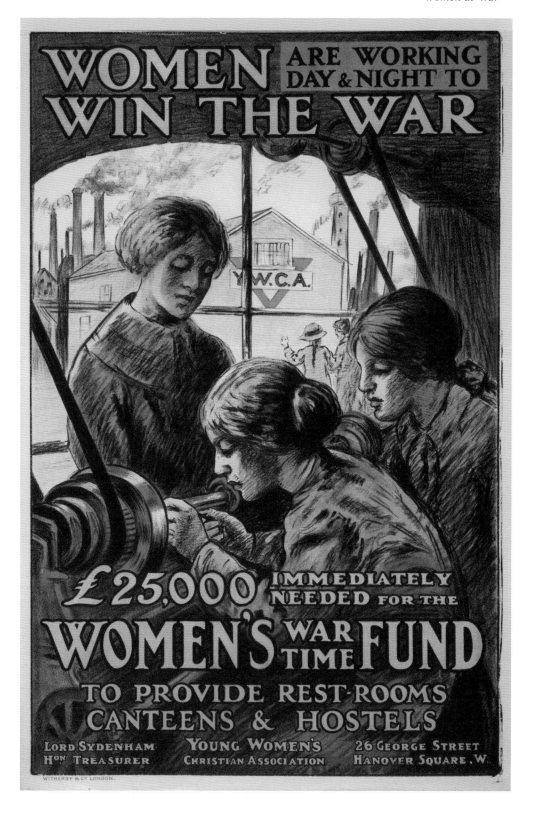

National Service poster promoting the Women's Land Army.

Family values. Published by His Majesty's Stationery Office, copies of this print by Harry Furniss could be purchased for 2*d*.

Daddy, what did _YOU_ do in the Great War?

PUBLISHED BY THE PARLIAMENTARY RECRUITING COMMITTEE, LONDON. POSTER NO. 79.   DESIGNED AND PRINTED BY JOHNSON, RIDDLE & CO., LTD., LONDON, S.E.

Daddy, what did YOU do in the Great War?
If not your wives, then your children could be used to apply the pressure. Three posters employing the tactic of provoking your shame at not answering the call on their behalf, and not just for now, but in the future as well. The famous 'Daddy' poster, *opposite*, was the brainchild of Paul Gunn of Johnson, Riddle & Co. printers. The story goes that the inspiration came to him one night after a discussion with his mother about whether he should volunteer. Gunn had artist Savile Lumley prepare the artwork with the scene projected forward to a few years after the war.

A PLAIN DUTY.

"WELL, GOODBYE, OLD CHAP, AND GOOD LUCK! I'M GOING IN HERE TO DO MY BIT, THE BEST WAY I CAN. THE MORE EVERYBODY SCRAPES TOGETHER FOR THE WAR LOAN, THE SOONER YOU'LL BE BACK FROM THE TRENCHES."

'A plain duty.' When this *Punch* cartoon was published, in February 1917, the war had almost two years still to run and the eventual outcome remained uncertain.

The War Machine

This intricately detailed poster was published in the later part of the war and explains 'How Great Britain has mobilised her industries'.

'Since the outbreak of war in August 1914, Great Britain has grappled with the task of "munitionment" with astonishing success, and to-day she is one great Arsenal. Not only has she maintained her armies at the Front with ever-increasing supplies, but she has also materially participated in the munitioning of her Allies. Despite the fact that more than five million men have been drafted to the Colours, she has raised a vast industrial army which is ceaselessly engaged upon the production of munitions. Her industries have been mobilised and placed upon a war footing, countless new factories have been erected, many old factories have been adapted for war purposes, and the output of munitions in the British Isles has been enormously increased. The workshops of Britain are at war, and they will know no truce until victory is secure.'

The individual panels provide the statistics. 'There are 2½ million persons engaged in Government work in munition trades, of whom nearly half a million are women.' Another states, 'In High Explosives the production is now more than 100 times what it was in January 1915.'

'Invest in the War Loan.' Doing your duty on the Home Front included dipping into your pocket to feed the war economy. Published by the Parliamentary War Savings Committee in July 1915.

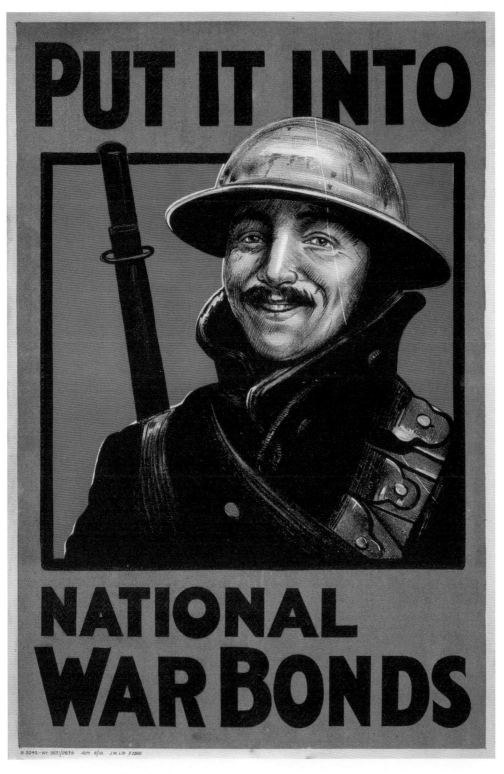

'Put it into National War Bonds.'

Left: The money might be needed for the war effort, but this poster is selling the concept of War Savings Certificates as an investment for the future. National War Savings Committee poster No. 35.

Bottom left: An appeal to common sense and the older men. Published in 1917.

Bottom right: 'An Appeal to Women' to put their savings into the war loan, dressed up with ribbons and white on blue cameos in the style of Wedgwood Jasperware.

Opposite: Poster published by the Parliamentary Recruiting Committee, with men listed after munitions. PRC poster No. 116.

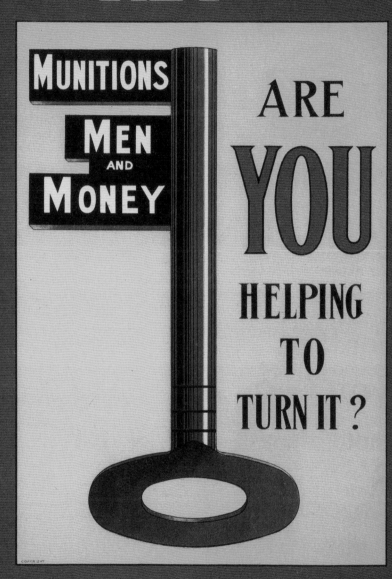

THE KEY TO THE

MUNITIONS
MEN AND MONEY

ARE YOU HELPING TO TURN IT?

SITUATION

Published by The Parliamentary Recruiting Committee, London. Poster No. 116   Printed by Spottiswoode Bros. Ltd. London & Aberdeen

Run-of-the-mill poster for war loans, with precious little graphic content or message, apart from 'Invest 5/- Today.'

Left: At least this poster makes some connection between the man at the Front and what you can do in the Post Office. For 15/6 (fifteen shillings and sixpence), you will eventually get £1 back. Published by the National Organising Committee.

Opposite: Lots of coins and a pound note, but no real impact.

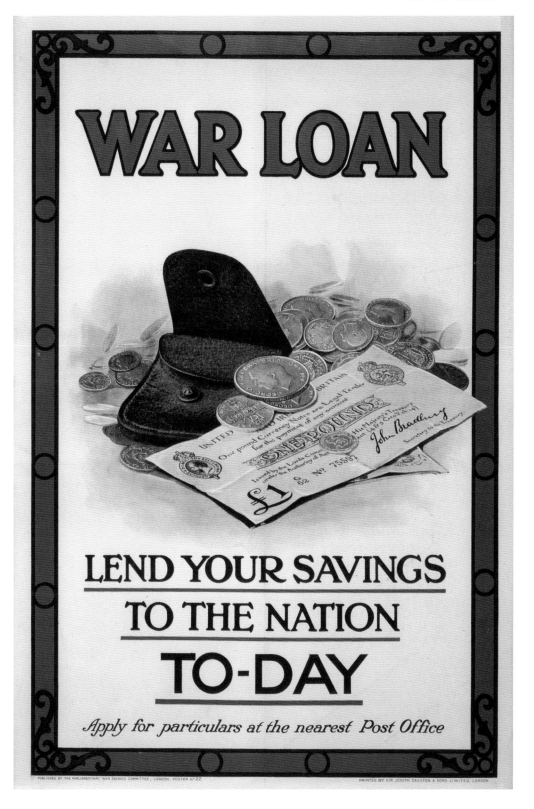

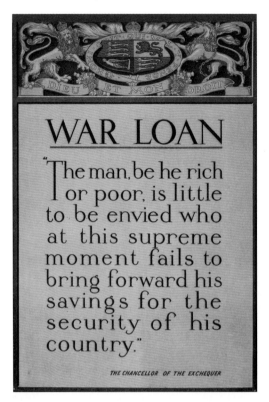

This page: Two more text-driven posters extolling the importance of the war loan and savings. The first is published by the Parliamentary War Savings Committee and brings us the words of the Chancellor of the Exchequer. The second is an advert for a booklet on 'Why we must save.'

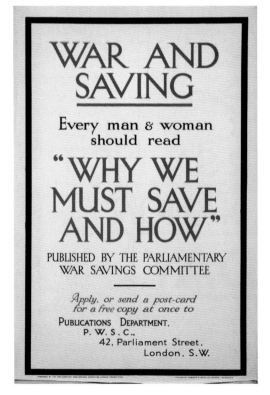

Opposite: At last a war savings poster that actually catches the eye, featuring a German – it appears to be the Kaiser – crushed by a mighty 1915 coin (presumably a crown coin which was worth five shillings).

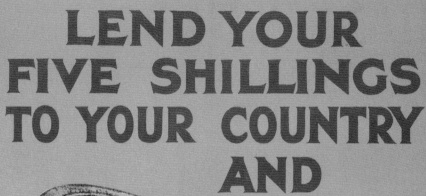

LEND YOUR
FIVE SHILLINGS
TO YOUR COUNTRY
AND

CRUSH
THE GERMANS

PUBLISHED BY THE PARLIAMENTARY WAR SAVINGS COMMITTEE, LONDON POSTER Nº23   PRINTED BY DAVID ALLEN & SONS Lᵈ HARROW, MIDDLESEX, W.G/12 40M·7/0

Left: Two war loan posters with representations of Saint George and King George, albeit on either side of a coin. The second one plays a pre-decimal pun on the sovereign as a coin (with a nominal value of one pound) as well as being the king.

Below: Another poster focussing on the financial aspect of War Savings Certificates.

Opposite: This clean graphic design by Bert Thomas looks remarkably undated and could just as well have come from the Second World War.

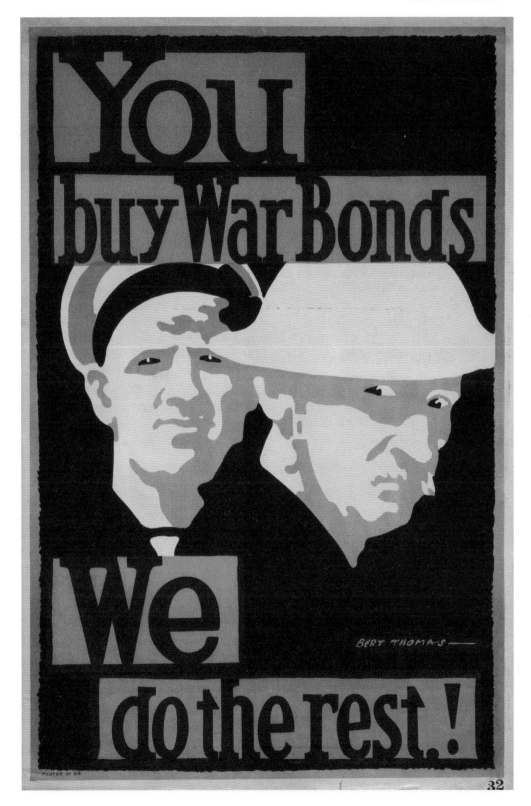

Buying War Savings Stamps meant you could spread the outlay and still lend your money to the war effort. Simple and unexciting perhaps, this poster does exactly what is required of it.

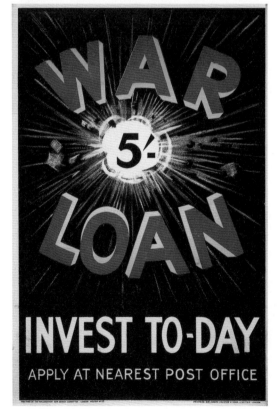

Left: 'War Loan.' An eye-catching but otherwise uninspiring poster published by the Parliamentary War Savings Committee.

Opposite: The lion as a symbol of Britain and the Empire has made remarkably few appearances in this selection of posters. Published by the Parliamentary War Savings Committee and printed in London. See also page 118.

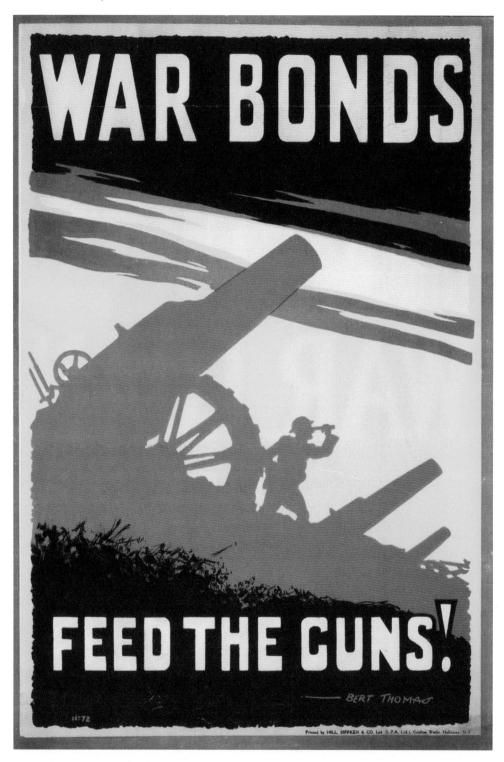

Bring on the big guns. Another strong design by Bert Thomas. No. 72 was printed in Holloway.

The tank was the wonder weapon of the First World War and its first successful use came at the Battle of Cambrai in late 1917. Tank tours within the UK were organised to sell War Bonds. This poster has a blank panel for the printer to add local details. Printed in Edinburgh.

THE SOLDIER AND THE MUNITION-WORKER.

"WE'RE BOTH NEEDED TO SERVE THE GUNS!"

[*With acknowledgments to a popular poster.*]

Above: 'We're both needed to serve the Guns!' We have seen several examples of cartoonists inspiring poster designs, but in this instance, the poster came first.

Left: The *Punch* cartoon, published in June 1915, puts Lloyd George and Lord Kitchener in the picture. After the shell crisis of 1915 he was appointed as Minister of Munitions. A year later he succeeded Lord Kitchener as Secretary of State for War following Kitchener's death aboard HMS *Hampshire*, which hit a mine on the way to Russia.

It wasn't just money that fed the war's insatiable demand for munitions. Skilled men were called upon to enrol for war work, and posters such these were produced to reinforce the message that they also played their part. It was only after the introduction of conscription under the Military Service Act of January 1916 that greater numbers of women were called upon in order to release the men to serve at the Front. Men in certain reserved occupations could apply for an exemption and their case was heard by a Military Service Tribunal. In some instances, such as with a farm worker at the time of harvest, they were given a deferment of service for a limited period. It is estimated that over 1 million men were in reserved occupations and they wore special badges to save them from the white feather brigade.

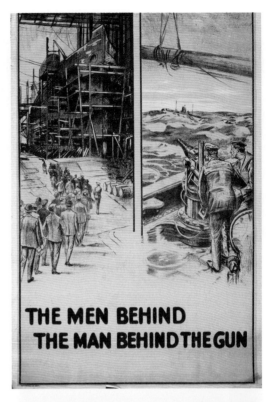

**THE MEN BEHIND
THE MAN BEHIND THE GUN**

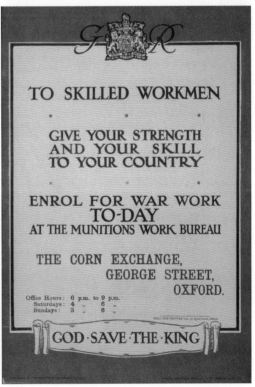

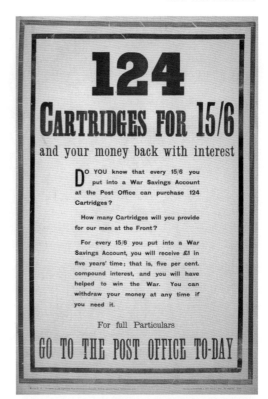

Opposite: Silver coins for bullets. Parliamentary War Savings Committee poster No. 19. Printed in London.

Right: '124 cartridges for 15/6.' This poster gives an unusually precise figure to show what your money will do for the war.

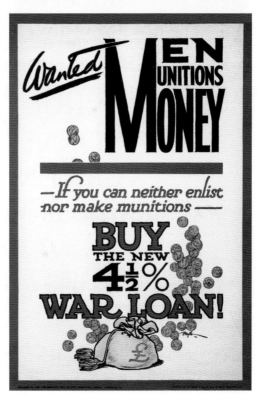

'Wanted – Men Munitions Money. If you can neither enlist nor make munitions buy the new 4½ % War Loan.'

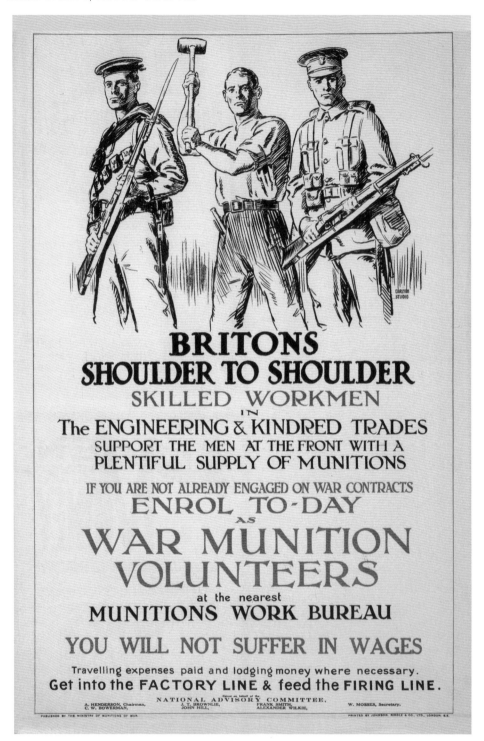

'Britons Shoulder to Shoulder' – a poster for War Munitions Volunteers which portrays the skilled workman on an equal basis with the sailor and soldier. Published by the Ministry of Munitions of War.

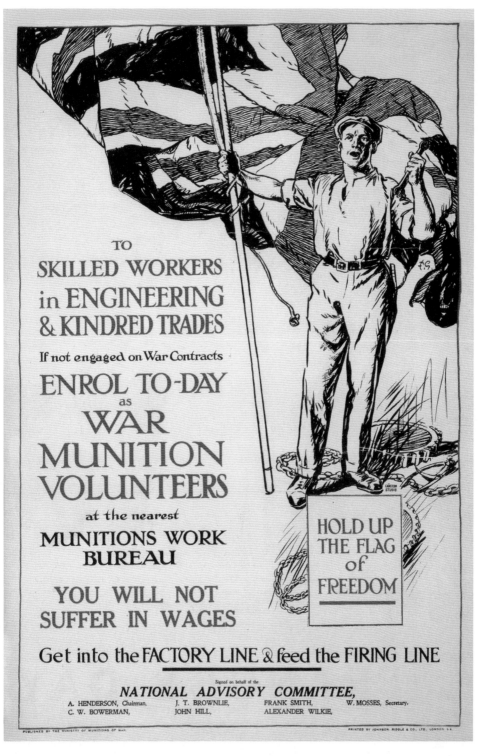

Another poster from the Ministry of Munitions of War. 'Get into the Factory Line and feed the Firing Line.'

For the French Red Cross

LONDON
COMMITTEE:
3 & 9 Knightsbridge
Hyde Park Corner
London · S.W.

Please Help

JULY
14

FRANCE'S DAY
IN AID OF THE FRENCH RED CROSS

A NATIONAL DEMONSTRATION of our cordial friendship with
our friend and ally, a tribute to the brave army of France and
a substantial proof of our sympathy with the wounded French soldiers

PLEASE SEND A CONTRIBUTION TO THE TREASURER, THE RIGHT HON. THE
LORD MAYOR OF LONDON, MANSION HOUSE, E.C.

W. H. SMITH & SON, THE ARDEN PRESS, STAMFORD STREET, LONDON, S.E.

15

Wartime Charities

By 1916 there were so many charities in Britain that Parliament passed the War Charities Act, which laid regulations for registration of charities, and a scheme to coordinate their efforts was instigated. Many of the charities published posters to raise awareness and, more importantly, funds in order to carry out their work. The character of these posters is very different to the bluntness of the recruiting posters, and it has been suggested that the more cultured women who ran the charities and committees were more likely to commission artists to design them. Hence the preponderance of guardian angels and saintly nurses. Their work tends to be far more illustrative and less graphic in its impact – more like art prints than posters. Judge for yourself.

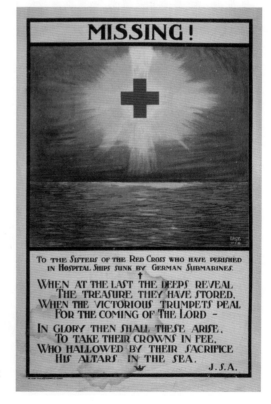

Opposite: France's Day in aid of the French Red Cross. Published by the London Committee.

Right: 'To the sisters of the Red Cross who have perished in hospital ships sunk by German submarines.'

Top left: Wetherby Flag Day, 1917, raising funds to erect huts on the Western Front for the Church Army. Artwork by John Hassall. See page 180.

Top right: 'Give and Heal.' Poster for the British Red Cross Day, published in Canada. 'For your stricken defenders on all the battle fronts.'

Bottom left: A locally printed poster for the Oxfordshire Red Cross Day.

Above: Frank Brangwyn's characteristically bold depiction of an ambulance on the Western Front. This design was made in 1918 for the *Daily Mail* and *Evening News* Red Cross Fund labels.

Right: Lamp Day, for 'Women's Service in War Time.'

The archetypical image of the nursing angel. Poster in aid of the Belgian Red Cross, copies were made available to purchase at one shilling.

Another Frank Brangwyn poster for another charitable cause, this time announcing 'The Remaking Belgium Exhibition' on behalf of the Belgium Town Planning Committee.

This page: Two posters designed by the artist John Hassall, who is better known for his advertising posters and illustrations for children's books. His most famous creation was the 'Jolly Fisherman', who appeared on the 'Skegness is SO bracing' poster for the Great Northern Railway. In 1900 Hassall had opened his own New Art School and School of Poster Design and his pupils included Bruee Bairnsfather, the creator of the Old Bill character who appeared in the First World War-era *Fragments from France*. The school was closed with the outbreak of the war.

'They must not starve' is a poster issued by the National Committee for Relief in Belgium, and the lower poster is for the Belgian Canal Boat Fund. There is another example of Hassall's work, 'Wetherby Flag Day' on page 176.

Opposite: Belgian Red Cross Fund poster by the Welsh artist and lithographer Gerald Spencer Pryse. He created his prints and posters by working directly on to lithographic stones. This style of dark, almost claustrophobic image, tightly cropped and energised by small splashes of bright colour, became his trademark for a series of posters produced for the Labour Party between the wars. A slightly more muted Pryse poster of the First World War era is shown on page 82.

In support of American servicemen fighting in the First World War the YMCA offered a range of services, including entertainment and recreational activities, rest programmes for the battle weary, and leave centres, as well as providing 4,000 huts for recreation and religious services, and some 1,500 canteens. Not strictly British of course, four of their posters are included because of their illustrative content of life on the Western Front and in London.

Above: YMCA motor kitchen in France, with artwork by Edgar Wright.

Below: YMCA poster, 'Services for relatives of dangerously wounded.' Also by Edgar Wright.

Above: '3 a.m. in a London Station Hut.' The YMCA had huts at several of London's main railway termini.

Below: 'A YMCA cellar in Flanders.'

16
The War Horses

In recent years the role of millions of horses in the First World War has been recognised through public memorials and has attracted widespread interest through Michael Morpurgo's *War Horse*, a story written for younger readers that subsequently took off as a stage show and then as a film by Stephen Spielberg (2011). In the early stages of the war, mounted warfare, that vestige of earlier conflicts (in particular the Boer War), was still seen as a viable means of attack. However, the mechanisation of warfare and the efficient dealing out of death by machine guns, resulting in the entrenchment of opposing positions, made the value of the cavalry charge highly questionable to most nations. The high casualties incurred – the German machine gunners would target the horses – didn't deter the British, who persisted with mounted infantry and cavalry offensives throughout the war.

For the poster artists these glorious charges provided some much needed drama, as in the example of a cavalry officer charging with sabre drawn shown on the opposite page. The horses had another important task and, at a time when motorised transport was still very much in its infancy, they were the most efficient means of pulling the big guns, moving munitions and supplies, and sending messages through the difficult and muddy terrain. It has been estimated that in total around 6 million horses took part in the war, and a million died on the British side alone. To lose a horse was worse than losing a man because men were replaceable. To meet the demand for horses, special breeding programmes were instigated and thousands of horses were confiscated from British civilians. Feeding the horses put an additional strain on the supply train and their waste and rotting carcasses added to the risk of disease. Many of the soldiers developed close bonds with their animals and they were shocked when, at the end of the war, the surfeit of horses saw thousands of animals sold off to the locals, many of them destined for the slaughterhouses.

Opposite: PRC poster No. 133.

AT THE FRONT!

Every fit Briton should join our brave men at the Front.

ENLIST NOW.

A team of six horses pulling a field gun. PRC poster No. 84.

The plight of the horses was recognised by charities such as Blue Cross Fund for Wounded Horses. No glorious charges here, just a riderless horse in distress.

STAR & GARTER HOME

for

TOTALLY DISABLED SOLDIERS AND SAILORS

PATRONS: H.M. THE QUEEN & H.M. QUEEN ALEXANDRA

Haven

Reproduced by permission of the Proprietors from Mr. Punch's Appeal for the Star and Garter Fund.

You can never repay these utterly broken men. But you can show your gratitude by helping to build this Home, where they will be tenderly cared for during the rest of their lives.

LET EVERY WOMAN SEND WHAT SHE CAN TO-DAY to the Lady Cowdray, Hon. Treasurer, The British Women's Hospital Fund, 21 Old Bond Street, W

Special Reproductions of the Cartoon, 2/6 and 1/-, can be obtained at above address, or, Postage and Packing free, 2/10 and 1/2

Postscript

It is impossible to measure the importance or impact of the British posters in the First World War. To many commentators the system of individual printers producing designs, which were then rubber-stamped by the Parliamentary Recruiting Committee, resulted in an output that was both uncoordinated and mediocre. In comparison with those of the other participants, they lacked artistic merit. The German posters, for example, relied on bold imagery with a clear message, while those of France followed in that country's tradition of art posters. A century later we have all become far more sophisticated in interpreting a prodigious and constant flow of images in our daily lives, and in reviewing the posters from the First World War it is hard to see them with the more innocent eyes of those times. These posters were about selling the war to the British public and constantly engaging them in a 'total' war that would only be won through the mathematics of an unending supply of men and munitions. The stark reality was that by the end of the war, the military and civilian casualties of the participating countries amounted to over 37 million, making it the deadliest conflict in human history. According to official figures Britain had lost 886,939 men through military deaths and a further 1,663,435 were wounded. Civilian deaths resulting from military action were in the region of 2,000.

By the time of the Second World War – sometimes regarded as the second round in one big global conflict – the immediate introduction of conscription rendered the recruitment poster redundant. Instead, the posters were much more orientated towards public information, conserving resources, doing your bit, raising funds and, in the age of wireless communication, a greater emphasis was placed on avoiding careless talk. And with regular wireless and newspaper reports on the progress of war, the public of the Second World War was far better informed than their First World War counterparts. They kept calm and carried on.

Opposite: The consequences of the conflict continued long after the fighting had finished. The poster for the Star & Garter Home for 'Totally Disabled Soldiers and Sailors' features another drawing from *Punch*. It is interesting to note that special reproductions of the cartoon could be purchased to raise funds.

An exhibition of recruiting posters in Russia. The large central poster is shown on page 168. Several of the smaller posters are also identifiable. (J&C McCutcheon Collection)

Bibliography

Barnicoat, John, *A Concise History of Posters* (Thames & Hudson, 1972).

Darracott, Joseph and Belinda Loftus, *First World War Posters* (Imperial War Museum, 1972).

Rickards, Maurice, *Posters of the First World War* (Evelyn, Adams & Mackay, 1968).

Rickards, Maurice and Michael Moody, *The First World War – Ephemera, Mementoes, Documents* (Jupiter Books, 1975).

Acknowledgements

My thanks go to the people and organisations that have contributed to this book: The images of the posters come from the US Library of Congress. Contemporary photographs and postcard images are from the J&C McCutcheon Collection, and the cartoons are from the author's collection.

JC

Also available from Amberley Publishing

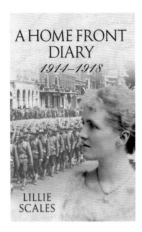

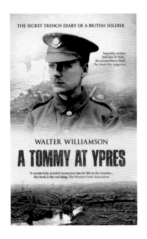
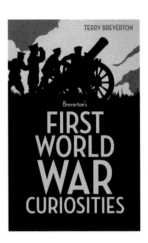